FUTURE R...

Vol. 1

HOW PLANET + CONSCIOUS = PLANECIOUS LEADERS ARE SHAPING A SUSTAINABLE WORLD

TRANSFORMATIVE LESSONS FROM GLOBAL VISIONAIRIES FOR THE NEXT GENERATION OF BUSINESS LEADERS

ROHIT KORAT

ISBN
Paperback 979-8-89588-960-2
Hardcase 979-8-89673-430-7

Contents

Introduction: A New Era of Sustainable Leadership for All Businesses

The world is undergoing a profound transformation. Climate change, resource depletion, and societal inequalities are reshaping the expectations placed on businesses. Organisations—whether large corporations, MSMEs, or non-profits—can no longer afford to focus solely on financial growth. There's a growing imperative to balance profits with purpose, ensuring that business strategies align with the well-being of people and the planet.

Sustainability has evolved from being a mere option to a necessity. Whether you are steering a global enterprise, leading a non-profit, or navigating the unique challenges of a micro, small, or medium-sized enterprise (MSME), sustainability provides a roadmap to future-proofing your operations. It is more than a compliance measure—it is a catalyst for innovation, growth, and long-term success.

Enter the era of *Planecious* leadership. Coined from the fusion of 'planet' and 'conscious,' the term represents a new breed of leaders who prioritise environmental stewardship while championing innovation and profitability. These leaders recognise that tackling today's global challenges is not just a moral responsibility but a strategic advantage. By embodying this ethos, they are reshaping industries, redefining success, and driving meaningful change.

This book invites you to explore the journeys of such trailblazers, offering tools, insights, and strategies that transcend organisational boundaries. You'll uncover ways to align your objectives with sustainable practices, build resilience, and unlock untapped potential for growth. From leveraging ESG reporting and harnessing innovative technologies to embracing the principles of a circular economy, the path to sustainability is diverse and dynamic.

The stories and strategies shared here are more than a guide—they are an invitation for you to become a *Planecious* leader yourself. By integrating purpose into your business framework, you not only ensure a thriving future for your organisation but also contribute to a planet that can sustain future generations. The journey starts now, with you.

Why Sustainability Matters for All Organisations

The pressure on businesses to integrate sustainability is mounting from all sides. Consumers are demanding more transparency, investors are favouring companies with strong environmental and social governance (ESG) practices, and governments are imposing stricter regulations around emissions and resource use. However, these shifts present a unique opportunity for forward-thinking businesses to lead with purpose, transforming challenges into strategic advantages.

For large corporations, this means scaling sustainability across global supply chains, adopting renewable energy, and leading through robust ESG frameworks. For MSMEs, it's about embracing their agility to innovate quickly, reduce emissions, and tap into the emerging carbon credit market. Non-profits and NGOs, on the other hand, are in a powerful position to advocate for sustainable practices and bridge the gap between businesses, communities, and policymakers.

Overview of the Chapters

This book provides a holistic exploration of sustainability across various sectors and business sizes. Here is a brief look at each chapter and what you can expect:

Chapter 1: The Rise of Purpose-Driven Innovation

The business world is evolving beyond profit, driven by leaders like Sunny Revankar who prove that sustainability and profitability can go hand-in-hand. Explore how groundbreaking approaches in ESG are not just changing industries but paving a path for ethical, impactful growth.

Chapter 2: Navigating the ESG Reporting Landscape

Transparency and accountability are the cornerstones of modern business success. Discover the intricacies of ESG frameworks, the challenges companies face in reporting, and how leveraging these tools can transform regulatory obligations into competitive advantages.

Chapter 3: Building a Sustainable Future—Insights from Industry Leaders

What does it mean to lead in sustainability? From tackling global challenges to embedding eco-conscious practices, delve into transformative stories from industry visionaries who have turned sustainability into a core element of their business strategies.

Chapter 4: A Zero-Waste Revolution

Can a simple pen redefine sustainability? Join Saurabh Mehta's journey as he transforms a wasteful industry with the world's first plastic-free pen, illustrating how even small innovations can lead to monumental environmental impacts.

Chapter 5: Bridging Disciplines for a Sustainable Future

The solution to global issues like water scarcity lies in collaboration. Mohammed Mahmoud's cross-disciplinary approach showcases how partnerships between businesses, governments, and experts are crucial for addressing climate challenges while fostering resilience.

Chapter 6: A Journey into Sustainability—Energy Efficiency and Beyond

From energy audits to renewable initiatives, Karunakar Avuram's transformative work proves that energy-intensive industries can be key players in reducing carbon footprints. Learn how technical expertise and visionary leadership drive meaningful change.

Chapter 7: Pioneers of a Sustainable Future

Meet the leaders reshaping the global sustainability narrative. Through innovation and a relentless commitment to their values, these pioneers inspire businesses to make a lasting impact while meeting the demands of a changing world.

Chapter 8: The Circular Economy in Action

Rethink waste as a resource in a world where circular economies redefine success. Discover how businesses are turning the linear "take-make-dispose" model on its head to create sustainable, regenerative systems that benefit everyone.

Chapter 10: Empowering Communities and Building a Sustainable Future

Tomorrow's sustainability leaders are being nurtured today. Learn how mentoring, education, and strategic empowerment prepare young minds to tackle pressing challenges and ensure business innovation thrives in the face of adversity.

Chapter 11: Overcoming Resistance to Change in Sustainability

Implementing green practices is often met with opposition, but success lies in fostering a culture of adaptability. Discover strategies to overcome resistance, build momentum, and embrace sustainability as an essential aspect of modern business.

Chapter 12: Tapping into the Carbon Credit Market

Carbon credits are transforming industries, offering financial rewards for eco-conscious choices. Explore how businesses, especially MSMEs, can harness this market to reduce emissions and unlock new revenue streams.

Chapter 13: Measuring and Communicating Sustainability Impact

In a world demanding transparency, the ability to measure and share progress is critical. Dive into best practices for tracking metrics, crafting compelling sustainability reports, and building stakeholder trust through accountability.

Sustainability: The Competitive Edge for All Businesses

As we navigate this new era of business transformation, it's clear that sustainability is no longer a 'nice-to-have' but a **competitive edge**. For corporations, it offers the ability to scale sustainable practices globally, attracting long-term investors and consumer loyalty. For MSMEs, sustainability opens the door to new markets, operational efficiency, and innovation. Non-profits and NGOs, meanwhile, have the unique ability to foster collaboration between businesses, communities, and governments, ensuring that sustainability goals are met on a societal level.

The strategies outlined in this book are designed to help all organisations—regardless of size—align their business models with the demands of a sustainable future. Whether you are just beginning your sustainability journey or looking to deepen your existing initiatives, this book will equip you with the knowledge, tools, and inspiration to lead with purpose and profit.

A Call to Action for Leaders Across All Sectors

The world is changing rapidly, and the time for businesses to act is now. Whether you are the CEO of a multinational corporation, a start-up founder, or a leader of a non-profit, the shift towards sustainability presents both a challenge and an opportunity. By integrating sustainability into your core business strategies, you not only reduce your environmental footprint but also unlock new growth opportunities, enhance your reputation, and build resilience for the future.

As you read through the chapters, you will see that sustainability is not just a responsibility—it's a business strategy for success in the 21st century. Let this book be your guide as you navigate the evolving landscape of sustainability, turning challenges into opportunities and setting the stage for a brighter, more sustainable future for all.

Chapter 1:
The Rise of Purpose-Driven Innovation

Overview: A New Era of Business Transformation

In today's fast-paced world, businesses are no longer judged by profits alone. Success now means stepping up to tackle global challenges like climate change, resource scarcity, and social inequality. This shift is fuelled by **purpose-driven innovation** – an approach that not only focuses on financial returns but also on creating a positive impact on society and the planet.

Purpose-driven innovation is about finding solutions that serve both people and the planet. It's where profitability meets sustainability, and it calls for businesses to rethink how they operate. Companies that embrace this shift are proving something revolutionary: you can grow, innovate, and thrive by aligning with values that matter to consumers, investors, and society at large.

In this chapter, we explore the story of **Sunny Revankar**, a trailblazer in Environmental, Social, and Governance (ESG) reporting. Sunny's journey showcases how purpose-driven innovation can disrupt traditional business models and pave the way for a more sustainable and successful future.

Sunny Revankar's Journey: From Civil Engineer to ESG Advocate

Sunny's path to sustainability leadership is one that's sure to inspire professionals and entrepreneurs alike. Starting as a civil engineer, Sunny was always drawn to the environmental and social aspects of infrastructure projects. His early work gave him a deep understanding of the environmental impacts tied to construction—everything from managing water resources to waste disposal. These experiences laid the foundation for his passion for sustainability.

But Sunny didn't stop there. His interest in the financial side of sustainability emerged during his MBA, where he discovered how companies could use sustainable finance to raise funds while minimising risk. This blend of environmental awareness from his civil engineering days and his newfound focus on finance gave Sunny a unique, holistic perspective on sustainability challenges and opportunities.

With experience in ESG ratings and sustainability disclosures, Sunny moved into leadership roles, helping companies navigate the often-complicated world of ESG reporting. At Stirrup Communications, he leads efforts to integrate ESG into core business strategies. For Sunny, this work isn't just about ticking regulatory boxes – it's about using purpose as a driver for innovation and long-term growth.

The Shift from Traditional Models: A New Business Imperative

For decades, businesses have focused on short-term profits, often ignoring the broader impact on society and the environment. Rooted in the Industrial Revolution, this old model prioritised extracting value from natural resources while minimising costs. While this approach fuelled economic growth, it also led to negative consequences—environmental degradation, depleted resources, and increased social inequality.

Sunny Revankar's work illustrates why this traditional model is quickly becoming outdated. He believes that the **future of business is inseparably linked to sustainability**—and those that fail to adapt will be left behind. The shift from traditional, profit-centric models to purpose-driven ones isn't just the right thing to do—it's the smart thing to do.

For Sunny, purpose-driven innovation means rethinking how businesses operate. It's no longer just about short-term gains. Companies need to focus on the long-term impact of their actions, from how they manage natural resources to how they treat employees and engage with communities. Businesses must create value for all stakeholders—not just shareholders—including the environment, customers, employees, and future generations.

A key area Sunny focuses on is **ESG reporting**. Through transparent and rigorous reporting, companies can measure and communicate their sustainability performance to investors, customers, and regulators. From tracking greenhouse gas emissions to assessing employee diversity, ESG metrics offer a comprehensive picture of a company's overall impact. This transparency builds trust with stakeholders and positions companies as sustainability leaders in their industry.

But **purpose-driven innovation** isn't just about reporting—it's about **innovation**. It's about rethinking traditional practices and embracing circular economy principles, where resources are reused, waste is minimised, and environmental impact is reduced. Sunny's work in **sustainable finance** shows how businesses can benefit financially from going green. By attracting investments through green bonds and ESG-linked loans, companies can gain access to lower interest rates and unlock financial advantages, all while doing good for the planet.

Conclusion: The Rise of Purpose-Driven Innovation

Sunny Revankar's journey represents the transformative shift from traditional business models to those built on purpose and innovation. His work shows that companies can no longer afford to ignore the environmental and social dimensions of their operations. By embracing **purpose-driven innovation**, businesses can not only disrupt outdated models but also meet the growing demand for sustainability, ensuring long-term success in a world that's constantly changing.

This chapter is just the beginning. As we move forward, we'll explore specific strategies, lessons, and case studies from leaders like Sunny, highlighting how integrating purpose with profit can solve global challenges and unlock new opportunities for businesses.

1. From Purpose to Profit: Aligning ESG with Business Success

Overview: In today's business landscape, success isn't just about profitability—it's about aligning purpose with profit. Sunny Revankar's journey shows how companies can use Environmental, Social, and Governance (ESG) principles to not only make a positive impact on the world but also drive financial growth.

Purpose as a Growth Driver

Sunny believes that businesses no longer have to choose between doing good and making money — they can do both. His work demonstrates how companies that embed purpose into their mission, particularly through ESG initiatives, create stronger connections with customers, employees, and investors. He emphasises that when a business commits to solving environmental challenges, it positions itself for long-term growth and resilience.

Example: Think of it as planting seeds for the future. By focusing on sustainability, companies are nurturing trust with stakeholders, which, in turn, leads to profitability. Sunny's work shows that businesses can flourish by turning purpose into a growth driver.

ESG Integration and Financial Performance

With a background in both civil engineering and finance, Sunny bridges the gap between sustainability and profitability. He used his MBA in finance to understand how companies can align ESG disclosures with financial performance. According to Sunny, integrating ESG metrics isn't just about meeting regulations—it's about building a solid foundation for long-term profitability and reducing risks.

Key Insight: For Sunny, ESG isn't a compliance exercise—it's a strategic asset. His message to entrepreneurs and leaders is clear: purpose-driven companies can outperform their peers by building resilience into their business models.

Sustainability as a Competitive Advantage

Sunny's work shows that companies with strong ESG performance have a competitive edge. Why? Because investors are increasingly looking for sustainable companies to back, customers are choosing brands that align with their values, and top talent is drawn to organisations with a clear purpose. Businesses that prioritise ESG build stronger relationships and create lasting value for all stakeholders.

Case Study: Sunny's work with sustainable finance is a prime example. By helping companies raise funds at lower interest rates through ESG-linked bonds and effective reporting, he shows how purpose and profit go hand-in-hand. His efforts prove that sustainable companies can unlock financial benefits while driving social and environmental change.

Key Takeaway for Readers: Purpose-driven innovation is not just a feel-good strategy—it's a smart business move. By integrating ESG into your business strategy, you're setting yourself up for long-term success while making a meaningful impact.

2. Case Study: ESG and Innovation in Corporate Reporting

Overview: Corporate reporting has evolved, and Sunny Revankar is at the forefront of this transformation. His work at Stirrup Communications demonstrates how companies are moving beyond traditional financial reporting to integrate ESG metrics that highlight their sustainability efforts.

The Evolution of ESG Reporting

In the past, corporate reporting was primarily focused on financial metrics. Today, however, the narrative has shifted. ESG metrics are now seen as equally critical to understanding a company's overall performance. Sunny has helped numerous organisations embrace this shift, ensuring their ESG reports reflect a commitment to environmental stewardship, social responsibility, and good governance.

Insight: Sunny emphasises that ESG reporting is about more than just checking boxes – it's about embedding transparency and accountability into the very fabric of the business. It's about showcasing your company's values to the world.

From Data to Action

Sunny's role is not just to help companies gather data, but to use that data to drive real, impactful business decisions. ESG reporting is a tool for assessing risk, uncovering opportunities, and improving operational resilience. Sunny helps companies take the data they collect and turn it into action plans that strengthen the business.

Example: Sunny points to the standardisation of key performance indicators (KPIs) as a critical step. Without standardised data, it's difficult for investors to compare companies effectively. By helping organisations adopt consistent ESG metrics, Sunny enables them to build trust with stakeholders and position themselves for success.

Key Takeaway for Readers: ESG reporting isn't a mere formality—it's an opportunity to build resilience, improve decision-making, and foster long-term value. By focusing on transparent and meaningful data, companies can build a stronger connection with their stakeholders.

3. Lessons for Entrepreneurs: Navigating the Future of ESG

Overview: For entrepreneurs and business leaders, the future is clear—ESG is no longer optional. Sunny Revankar offers practical advice on how start-ups and established businesses alike can navigate this new landscape by focusing on the fundamentals of ESG.

Building Internal Capacity for ESG

One of Sunny's key recommendations is for businesses to build internal teams dedicated to ESG data collection and reporting. This isn't just about gathering numbers – it's about embedding sustainability into the core of the company. Transparency is key, and a dedicated team ensures that ESG metrics are tracked and reported accurately.

The Role of Technology

In today's digital age, technology is transforming how companies manage their ESG efforts. From cloud-based data management tools to advanced analytics platforms, Sunny highlights how technology has made it easier for businesses to track, report, and improve their environmental and social metrics.

Materiality Assessments

Sunny emphasises the importance of materiality assessments, which help businesses identify the sustainability issues that matter most to their industry and stakeholders. These assessments ensure that companies focus their resources on what will have the biggest impact.

Case Study: Sunny shares how materiality assessments helped companies streamline their ESG reporting and align it with their business goals. By focusing on the most relevant issues, they were able to make informed decisions and enhance their performance.

Key Takeaway for Readers: To succeed in ESG, entrepreneurs must prioritise transparency, invest in the right technology, and focus on the issues that matter most to their business and stakeholders. Building internal capacity is key to driving long-term sustainability.

4. Action Plan: Implementing ESG as a Core Business Strategy

Overview: Sunny Revankar offers a practical step-by-step guide for organisations looking to adopt ESG as a core business strategy. By following these steps, businesses can build a strong foundation for sustainability and long-term growth.

Action Plan Steps:

1. **Start with Materiality Assessments:** Sunny stresses the importance of starting with materiality assessments to identify the most critical ESG risks and opportunities.

2. **Build an ESG Team:** Companies need a dedicated team to manage data collection, reporting, and sustainability initiatives. This team should work across departments to ensure collaboration.

3. **Adopt Global Standards:** Sunny advocates for adopting internationally recognised frameworks such as GRI, SASB, and BRSR to ensure transparency and accountability.

4. **Set Long-Term Sustainability Goals:** Businesses must set ambitious yet achievable goals—whether it's reducing carbon emissions, improving water management, or enhancing social equity.

5. **Engage Stakeholders:** Involving both internal and external stakeholders is crucial for shaping sustainability strategies.

6. **Leverage Technology:** Use digital tools for real-time ESG tracking and reporting to stay on top of sustainability data.

Key Takeaway for Readers: Implementing ESG requires a clear, methodical approach. Sunny's action plan provides a roadmap for businesses looking to integrate sustainability into their core operations and achieve lasting success.

5. Looking Ahead: The Future of ESG and Sustainability

Overview: Sunny Revankar believes the future of business is deeply intertwined with sustainability. As companies embrace ESG, they will unlock new opportunities for growth, innovation, and financial success.

ESG as a Driver of Innovation

ESG is no longer just a compliance measure – it's a catalyst for innovation. Sunny shares how businesses can use sustainability to fuel new ideas and transform their operations for the better.

The Growth of Sustainable Finance

Sustainable finance is on the rise, and Sunny predicts that companies with strong ESG performance will have better access to funding. ESG-linked bonds and investments are becoming mainstream, offering businesses a powerful tool to attract capital.

Global Impact of ESG

Companies that adopt ESG practices are not only positioned for financial success – they're also contributing to global environmental and social progress.

Key Takeaway for Readers: The future belongs to businesses that embrace sustainability. Those who innovate and lead with purpose will not only thrive financially but also drive positive change on a global scale.

Conclusion: Purpose-Driven Innovation for a Sustainable Future

The rise of purpose-driven innovation is transforming the business world. As Sunny Revankar's journey shows, companies that integrate ESG into their strategy aren't just managing risk – they're unlocking new opportunities for growth, innovation, and long-term success.

Call to Action for Readers: Take inspiration from Sunny's journey and start integrating purpose-driven, sustainable practices into your business today. Whether you're a busy professional or a young entrepreneur, the time to act is now.

Chapter 2:

Navigating the ESG Reporting Landscape – Insights from Sunny Revankar

As the sustainability movement gains momentum, businesses find themselves at a crossroads: they can either integrate environmental, social, and governance (ESG) practices into their core strategy or risk falling behind. In this in-depth conversation with Sunny Revankar, a leading ESG consultant and advocate for sustainability, we explore how businesses can navigate the complexities of ESG reporting and translate these efforts into long-term value. Sunny's insights reflect the growing urgency for organisations to embrace sustainability, not as a compliance measure, but as a strategic driver of growth.

Building on the themes of purpose-driven innovation introduced in his first interview, this chapter delves deeper into the technical and operational challenges businesses face when implementing ESG frameworks. It also offers actionable insights for busy professionals and young entrepreneurs who are striving to balance short-term financial pressures with long-term sustainability goals. Sunny's examples and case studies provide a roadmap for leaders looking to make an authentic impact while navigating the fast-evolving landscape of ESG reporting.

Embracing the Complexity of ESG Consulting: A New Phase of Evolution

In Sunny's first interview, we explored how ESG is transforming business by linking purpose with profit. This second conversation, however, reflects the complexities that have arisen as more companies begin to adopt sustainability practices. With governments introducing more stringent regulations and stakeholders demanding greater transparency, businesses are no longer grappling with whether to implement ESG strategies—but how.

"Each organisation has a unique set of ESG consulting needs," Sunny explains. He notes that even within the same sector, companies face distinct challenges. For example, a manufacturing firm's focus might be on environmental compliance and reducing emissions, while a financial institution may need to address governance issues like ethical investing or diversity in leadership. These nuances make it clear that one-size-fits-all approaches to ESG no longer suffice.

A notable development Sunny highlighted is the growing importance of **BRSR (Business Responsibility and Sustainability Reporting)** in India. SEBI (Securities and Exchange Board of India) introduced BRSR as a regulatory framework that demands rigorous reporting from the top 1000 companies. "It's no longer just about ticking boxes; these companies are now held accountable in very specific ways," Sunny elaborates. For example, companies must now disclose purchasing power parity and segregate employment data by rural and urban regions, forcing businesses to be transparent about their broader societal impact.

Key Insight: Sunny's message is clear—businesses must embrace these changes not as roadblocks but as opportunities to innovate. As the regulatory landscape becomes more complex, those who can adapt will emerge as leaders in their field.

Case Study: Guiding a Major Bank Through the ESG Maze

One of the most illustrative examples of Sunny's work is a recent project he led with a large Indian bank. This bank, with its expansive nationwide reach, was determined to meet ESG requirements but lacked the necessary resources and time to gather the necessary data. Their initial goal was to comply with GRI (Global Reporting Initiative) standards, but due to internal delays, they fell short.

"When the client has the will, it makes it easier," Sunny explains, "but even with the best intentions, many organisations don't realise the complexity of gathering accurate data." The project involved collaborating across departments like HR and manufacturing to extract data points for ESG reporting. From employee diversity metrics to energy consumption figures, Sunny's team needed to guide the bank through every step of the process.

One significant challenge arose around calculating the lost-time injury rate (LTIR), a metric used to assess workplace safety. If miscalculated, this figure could easily be rejected at the assurance stage, affecting the bank's overall ESG score. Additionally, the bank wanted to merge its Scope 1 and Scope 2 emissions data, but Sunny had to explain that under BRSR guidelines, these categories must be reported separately.

"This kind of project illustrates why ESG consulting is more than just data collection—it's about knowing the intricacies of each reporting framework and guiding the client through them," Sunny notes. By engaging with the bank's leadership and educating key departments, Sunny's team was able to ensure compliance and help the bank meet its sustainability goals.

The Misconception Around ESG Ratings: Addressing the Real Challenge

One of the most common mistakes Sunny encounters in his line of work is the assumption that better ESG data will automatically lead to higher ESG ratings. "There's this misconception that simply improving the data will improve the rating," he says. This reflects a more significant misunderstanding of how ESG ratings actually work.

Sunny breaks it down: ESG rating agencies, such as MSCI and Sustainalytics, use two primary models to evaluate companies—the subscriber-pay model and the issuer-pay model. Each model relies on different criteria for rating an organisation's ESG performance. "Even if you're not actively seeking a rating, your ESG score can still be assessed based on publicly available information," Sunny warns. This is a critical insight for businesses unaware that their ESG performance is being scrutinised even if they don't directly participate in rating exercises.

Furthermore, in India, SEBI has authorised several rating agencies to assess companies specifically on their BRSR performance. This makes it essential for companies to focus on BRSR compliance if they want to improve their India-specific ESG scores. But improving these scores is not as simple as submitting better data. Sunny emphasises that companies must align with a consistent reporting framework—be it GRI, CDP, or BRSR—and ensure that the data they provide is transparent and complete.

Key Insight: The methodology used by ESG rating agencies is fixed, and businesses must work within these frameworks if they want to improve their ESG ratings. Incomplete or inconsistent data submissions can lead to poor ratings even if a company is performing well in terms of sustainability. This insight underscores the need for businesses to treat ESG reporting as a strategic asset, not a box-ticking exercise.

Double Materiality: Understanding the Broader Financial and Social Impact

In our first conversation with Sunny, we discussed how purpose-driven companies can outperform their peers by aligning their operations with long-term sustainability goals. Building on that theme, Sunny introduces a more nuanced concept in this interview: **double materiality**.

Double materiality refers to the idea that companies must consider both the internal and external impacts of their actions. In other words, ESG reporting isn't just about how environmental or social factors affect the company itself – it's about how these factors affect broader society and, in turn, the company's financial performance.

"Double materiality looks at two sides of the coin," Sunny explains. "On one hand, you have environmental and social risks that could affect your operations, and on the other, you have to assess how your business impacts those external factors." This expanded perspective is becoming increasingly relevant, especially in sectors like manufacturing, energy, and finance.

Sunny offers a practical example to illustrate this point. Suppose a manufacturing company is heavily reliant on water for its production processes. Under a traditional ESG approach, the company would assess how water scarcity might impact its ability to operate. Under double materiality, however, the company would also need to consider how its water consumption affects local communities and ecosystems. This broader understanding could help the company make more informed decisions about water management, potentially mitigating both financial and social risks.

In practice, double materiality can also help companies identify new business opportunities. For instance, a company that reduces its carbon footprint through innovative technologies may not only lower its operational risks but also position itself as a leader in sustainability— attracting investment and gaining a competitive edge.

Case Study: Reducing Risk in the Cement Industry

Sunny highlights a case study from the cement industry, where double materiality has been critical to managing both operational risks and societal impacts. Cement production is notorious for its high carbon emissions, which not only contribute to climate change but also expose companies to financial risks in a world moving towards stricter emissions regulations.

In this case, the company in question faced significant risks due to rising carbon costs. However, by adopting a double materiality approach, they also recognised the broader environmental impact of their operations. As a result, the company invested in new carbon capture technology, which not only reduced its emissions but also lowered its long-term financial risks. Moreover, the move positioned the company as a leader in green innovation, opening up new avenues for investment and growth.

Key Takeaway for Readers: Double materiality offers businesses a more comprehensive view of both risks and opportunities. By considering the external impact of their operations, companies can make more informed decisions, reduce long-term risks, and identify new growth opportunities.

Engaging Employees in Sustainability: From Awareness to Action

While top-down leadership is essential for driving ESG initiatives, Sunny emphasises the importance of engaging employees at every level of the organisation. "Employees are the lifeblood of any sustainability effort," he notes. This aligns with his earlier message that companies must embed purpose into their operations, not just their branding.

Sunny shares several examples of how companies are successfully involving employees in their sustainability efforts. One company, for instance, rolled out an initiative to reduce energy consumption by replacing traditional lighting systems with low-energy LED lights. Employees were actively involved in the process—tracking their department's energy usage and brainstorming ways to further reduce consumption.

Another example comes from the CSR (Corporate Social Responsibility) sector, where companies encourage employees to participate in biodiversity conservation projects. One such project focused on the protection of mangrove forests, which play a crucial role in carbon sequestration and protecting coastal ecosystems. By involving employees in these efforts, the company not only strengthened its CSR credentials but also built a stronger connection between its workforce and its sustainability mission.

Key Takeaway for Readers: To build a truly sustainable company, ESG must be more than a management directive—it must be a shared mission that involves everyone from the C-suite to the factory floor. Engaging employees in sustainability initiatives fosters a sense of ownership and accountability, making ESG an integral part of the company culture.

The Future of ESG Reporting: Leveraging Technology for Better Transparency

In this digital age, technology is revolutionising the way companies manage their ESG reporting. As ESG reporting becomes more standardised, the use of technology—particularly SaaS (Software as a Service) platforms—allows companies to collect, manage, and report their data more efficiently.

Sunny explains that SaaS-based tools provide real-time tracking of ESG metrics, enabling companies to monitor their sustainability performance continuously. These tools reduce the risk of human error and make it easier to comply with reporting standards. "We're moving towards a world where ESG data is managed digitally and in real-time, which will improve transparency across the board," Sunny says.

A prime example of this is a company Sunny worked with in the manufacturing sector. The company implemented a SaaS tool to track its GHG emissions across multiple plants. Instead of manually collecting data from each location, plant managers were given access to the tool, allowing them to input data in real-time. This system reduced the time spent on reporting by 50% and significantly improved data accuracy. Moreover, the tool's automated analysis functions provided instant insights into how different plants were performing, enabling the company to make quicker decisions about where to focus its sustainability efforts.

Balancing Short-Term Financial Pressures with Long-Term Sustainability Goals

One of the most pressing challenges companies face is balancing short-term financial demands with long-term sustainability goals. In today's competitive marketplace, many businesses struggle to justify the upfront costs of implementing sustainable practices, especially during periods of economic uncertainty. However, Sunny stresses that long-term thinking is crucial to building a resilient business model.

Sunny advises companies to approach sustainability as a gradual process. "You can't switch everything overnight," he says, pointing out that even small changes can have a significant impact over time. For example, he cites the case of a company that initially replaced plastic packaging with recyclable materials. Although the transition increased costs by 7%, it ultimately led to higher customer satisfaction and increased sales because the company's products appealed to eco-conscious consumers.

By taking a phased approach to sustainability, companies can make incremental improvements without jeopardising their financial stability. Sunny also highlights the importance of securing stable ESG budgets to ensure that long-term sustainability projects remain on track, even during periods of economic downturn.

Key Takeaway for Readers: Sustainability doesn't have to come at the expense of short-term profitability. By making incremental changes and taking a long-term view, companies can align their financial goals with their ESG objectives, creating a win-win scenario.

Conclusion: Building a Future-Ready Business Through ESG

Sunny Revankar's journey, from his early work in ESG consulting to his current role as a leader in the field, underscores the importance of aligning sustainability with long-term business strategy. His insights offer a clear roadmap for professionals and entrepreneurs looking to integrate ESG into their operations. The path forward is not without challenges, but as Sunny's case studies and examples demonstrate, the rewards far outweigh the risks.

By embracing double materiality, engaging employees, leveraging technology, and balancing short-term financial pressures with long-term sustainability goals, businesses can build resilience, drive innovation, and unlock new opportunities for growth.

Key Takeaways for Readers:

1. **Leverage Double Materiality**: Take a comprehensive approach to sustainability by considering both the financial and social impacts of your operations.

2. **Engage Employees**: Make sustainability a shared mission across the entire organisation. Involve employees at every level to foster a culture of responsibility and accountability.

3. **Use Technology to Drive Transparency**: Adopt SaaS-based tools to track and manage ESG data in real-time, improving accuracy and transparency.

4. **Think Long-Term, Act Incrementally**: Balancing short-term financial pressures with long-term sustainability goals is essential. Start with small changes and build from there.

5. **ESG is a Strategic Asset**: Treat ESG reporting as a critical part of your business strategy, not just a

compliance exercise. Transparency and consistency in reporting will lead to better performance and stronger stakeholder relationships.

By following these principles, companies can not only meet the growing demands of regulators and investors but also position themselves as leaders in the global movement towards sustainability.

Chapter 3:

Sustainable Innovation, Inclusive Leadership: Insights from Soumitra Purkayastha

In today's fast-evolving world, the need for sustainable growth and inclusive leadership has never been more pressing. For Soumitra Purkayastha, a visionary leader in the chemical industry, balancing these demands is not just an objective—it's a lifelong mission. From fostering innovation to supporting farmers, championing diversity, and promoting lifelong learning, Purkayastha's work is a testament to the power of purpose-driven leadership.

In a recent conversation, Purkayastha shared his insights on how businesses can navigate some of the biggest challenges of our time. With a career rooted in the chemical industry, his experiences offer valuable lessons for busy professionals and young entrepreneurs who are determined to create a more sustainable, inclusive future.

Sustainable Growth Through Innovation

When it comes to growth, Purkayastha is clear: sustainability must be at the core of any forward-thinking business. But achieving this goal isn't always easy, especially in an industry as resource-intensive as chemicals. According to Purkayastha, the key to driving sustainable growth lies in innovation. "Sustainability and innovation go hand-in-hand," he explained. "Without innovation, sustainability remains an ideal rather than a reality."

In his work, Purkayastha has always prioritised innovation as a driving force for change. "We can't keep doing things the way they've always been done," he said. "If we want to grow sustainably, we need to rethink everything—from the raw materials we use to how we manage waste."

One of the ways Purkayastha has done this is by investing in green chemistry – a field that seeks to reduce the environmental impact of chemical production. By exploring alternative, eco-friendly raw materials and minimising hazardous waste, Purkayastha has helped lead a shift in the industry towards more sustainable practices. This shift, however, isn't just about technology. For Purkayastha, it's about changing mindsets and encouraging teams to think differently.

"Innovation is as much about culture as it is about science," he said. "It's about fostering curiosity, encouraging people to ask questions, and being willing to take risks." This mindset has allowed him to push the boundaries of what's possible in chemical manufacturing, all while keeping sustainability at the forefront.

For professionals and entrepreneurs, this insight is crucial. Whether you're in chemicals, technology, or any other sector, sustainability is no longer a nice-to-have—it's a business imperative. But making it happen requires bold thinking and a commitment to innovation. Purkayastha's approach teaches us that sustainable growth isn't about quick fixes; it's about reimagining processes, investing in new technologies, and nurturing a culture of innovation.

Key Insight: Sustainable growth is driven by innovation. To achieve it, businesses must be willing to rethink traditional processes and foster a culture of curiosity and risk-taking.

Challenges in the Chemical Industry

The chemical industry, with its reliance on natural resources and high energy consumption, faces unique challenges when it comes to sustainability. For Soumitra Purkayastha, addressing these challenges requires a delicate balance between economic viability and environmental responsibility.

"The chemical industry is vital to so many sectors—agriculture, pharmaceuticals, manufacturing—but it's also one of the most resource-intensive," he noted. "Our challenge is to continue meeting the needs of these industries while minimising our environmental footprint."

One of the biggest obstacles, according to Purkayastha, is the complexity of supply chains. From sourcing raw materials to managing logistics and waste, the chemical industry's supply chains are vast and interconnected. "It's not just about what happens within your own company," he explained. "You need to consider the entire lifecycle of a product, from the raw materials you use to how it's disposed of at the end of its life."

This focus on lifecycle thinking has been central to Purkayastha's approach to sustainability. By adopting a more holistic view of chemical production, he has been able to identify areas where improvements can be made—not just within the company, but across the entire supply chain.

For busy professionals and entrepreneurs, this lesson is particularly relevant. In today's globalised economy, no business operates in isolation. Whether you're producing chemicals or running a tech start-up, the sustainability of your operations depends on the sustainability of your entire supply chain. By taking a step back and looking at the bigger picture, you can identify opportunities to reduce waste, improve efficiency, and create more sustainable business models.

Key Insight: In complex industries like chemicals, sustainability requires a holistic approach. Leaders must consider the entire lifecycle of their products and look for ways to reduce environmental impact across the supply chain.

Supporting Farmers: A Holistic Approach to Agricultural Sustainability

For Purkayastha, the link between the chemical industry and agriculture is deeply personal. As someone who has worked closely with farmers for much of his career, he understands the critical role that agriculture plays in feeding the world's growing population. However, he also recognises the challenges farmers face, from climate change to resource scarcity.

"Agriculture is at the heart of so many of the sustainability issues we're grappling with," he said. "Farmers are on the front lines of climate change, but they're also key to the solution."

Purkayastha has been a vocal advocate for supporting farmers, not just through the development of better agricultural chemicals, but by promoting sustainable farming practices. He believes that the chemical industry has a responsibility to help farmers adapt to changing environmental conditions by providing them with the tools and knowledge they need to succeed.

One example of this is his work on sustainable fertiliser development. By creating fertilisers that release nutrients more efficiently, Purkayastha has helped farmers increase crop yields while reducing the environmental impact of chemical runoff. But he knows that technology alone isn't enough. "It's not just about giving farmers better products," he explained. "We also need to provide them with education and support so they can implement sustainable practices on their farms."

For entrepreneurs and professionals in any industry, this holistic approach is a powerful lesson. Sustainability isn't just about developing innovative products or services – it's about empowering your customers, partners, and stakeholders to adopt sustainable practices. Whether you're working with farmers or tech users, providing education and support is key to driving long-term change.

Key Insight: Supporting sustainable growth in industries like agriculture requires a holistic approach. Businesses must provide both innovative products and the education needed to implement sustainable practices.

Diversity and Inclusion (D&I): Building Stronger Teams

In addition to his work in sustainability, Purkayastha is a passionate advocate for diversity and inclusion (D&I). For him, fostering a diverse and inclusive workplace isn't just about doing the right thing – it's about driving innovation and growth.

"Diversity is a strength," he said. "When you bring together people from different backgrounds, with different perspectives, you create an environment where creativity and innovation can thrive."

Purkayastha has been a champion of D&I throughout his career, leading initiatives to ensure that his teams are not only diverse in terms of gender and ethnicity but also in terms of ideas and experiences. "It's about creating a culture where everyone feels valued and heard," he explained. "When people feel like they belong, they're more engaged, more productive, and more willing to take risks."

For professionals and entrepreneurs, Purkayastha's message is clear: diversity and inclusion are not just HR buzzwords – they're essential to building strong, innovative teams. By fostering an inclusive culture where people feel empowered to contribute their unique perspectives, you can drive better decision-making, improve problem-solving, and ultimately achieve better business outcomes.

Key Insight: Diversity and inclusion are critical to innovation and growth. Leaders must create a culture where everyone feels valued and empowered to contribute.

LGBTQ+ Awareness and Inclusivity

A key aspect of Purkayastha's commitment to diversity and inclusion is his advocacy for LGBTQ+ awareness and inclusivity. In many industries, including chemicals, LGBTQ+ individuals often face barriers to full participation and inclusion. Purkayastha is determined to change that.

'We have to create environments where people can bring their whole selves to work,' he said. 'That means being intentional about LGBTQ+ inclusion—ensuring that policies, practices, and culture are all aligned to support and celebrate diversity.'

Purkayastha has led efforts within his organisation to create safe spaces for LGBTQ+ employees, from establishing employee resource groups to ensuring that company policies explicitly protect against discrimination based on sexual orientation and gender identity. But he knows that true inclusivity goes beyond policies. "It's about culture," he explained. "It's about making sure that everyone, from leadership to entry-level employees, understands and values the importance of LGBTQ+ inclusion."

For leaders and entrepreneurs, LGBTQ+ awareness and inclusivity are essential components of building a modern, progressive organisation. As Purkayastha's work demonstrates, fostering a truly inclusive environment requires more than just policies – it requires a commitment to building a culture of acceptance and respect.

Key Insight: LGBTQ+ awareness and inclusivity are critical to creating a supportive and diverse workplace.

Leaders must be intentional about building a culture where all employees feel valued and respected.

Curiosity and Lifelong Learning: The Fuel for Innovation

One of the key traits that has driven Purkayastha's success is his insatiable curiosity. For him, lifelong learning isn't just a nice-to-have—it's essential to staying relevant and innovative in a rapidly changing world.

"Curiosity is what drives innovation," he said. "It's about asking questions, exploring new ideas, and being open to change."

Throughout his career, Purkayastha has made it a priority to continually expand his knowledge, whether through formal education or simply by staying curious about the world around him. "Learning doesn't stop when you graduate from school," he said. "In fact, that's when it really begins. The world is constantly evolving, and if you want to stay ahead, you need to keep learning."

For professionals and entrepreneurs, this mindset is invaluable. In today's fast-paced business environment, where technology is constantly advancing and industries are being disrupted, the ability to learn and adapt is critical to success. Purkayastha's commitment to lifelong learning serves as a reminder that no matter how experienced or successful you are, there is always more to learn.

Key Insight: Lifelong learning is essential to staying relevant and innovative. Leaders must foster a culture of curiosity and continuous growth.

Balancing Population Growth with Sustainability

One of the biggest challenges facing the world today is how to balance population growth with sustainability. As the global population continues to rise, the demand for resources—food, water, energy—will only increase. For Purkayastha, this is one of the most pressing issues of our time.

"The challenge is clear," he said. "We need to find ways to meet the needs of a growing population without depleting the planet's resources."

Purkayastha believes that innovation is the key to solving this challenge. Whether it's developing more efficient agricultural practices, creating renewable energy sources, or finding new ways to manage waste, innovation will play a critical role in balancing population growth with sustainability. But, as he points out, innovation alone isn't enough. "We also need to be smart about how we manage our resources," he said. "That means reducing waste, improving efficiency, and making sure that we're using our resources in a way that benefits both people and the planet."

For professionals and entrepreneurs, the challenge of balancing population growth with sustainability offers a unique opportunity to innovate. Whether you're working in agriculture, energy, or any other industry, there are countless ways to contribute to a more sustainable future. The key is to think creatively and be willing to embrace new ideas and technologies.

Key Insight: Balancing population growth with sustainability requires innovation and resource management. Leaders must find creative ways to meet the needs of a growing population while protecting the planet.

Conclusion: A Call to Action for Future Leaders

Soumitra Purkayastha's journey offers invaluable lessons for professionals and entrepreneurs who are passionate about sustainability, innovation, and inclusivity. From his commitment to supporting farmers and driving diversity to his advocacy for LGBTQ+ awareness and his focus on lifelong learning, Purkayastha's leadership is rooted in the belief that sustainable growth requires both innovation and inclusivity.

As we move forward, his message is clear: the challenges we face—whether in sustainability, diversity, or population growth—are complex, but they are not insurmountable. With curiosity, collaboration, and a commitment to continuous learning, we can create a future that is not only sustainable but also inclusive and equitable for all.

Now is the time for all of us to take action. Whether you're leading a team, building a business, or simply looking to make a difference in your community, remember that your efforts matter. Together, we can drive the innovation and inclusivity needed to build a better future for everyone.

Chapter 4:

A Zero-Waste Revolution: Saurabh Mehta's Journey to Creating the World's First Plastic-Free Pen

The Genesis of NOTE: Turning a Problem Into a Solution

Rohit: Saurabh, thank you for joining us today. Could you start by telling us the story behind founding NOTE and your vision for creating the world's first plastic-free pen?

Saurabh: Absolutely, Rohit. Thanks for having me! The idea for **NOTE** came from a very personal realisation. I've been involved in the sustainability space for over 15 years, but it wasn't until 2016, when I joined my family's business in Delhi, that I saw the problem right in front of me. The business was in plastic ballpoint pens—disposable pens, or as some call them, *use-and-throw* pens. That terminology itself struck me as problematic. These pens, meant for education, were essentially throwaway items, contributing to massive amounts of waste.

The issue with pens is that they contain so many different parts – plastic, metal, rubber, zinc springs – that make recycling almost impossible. Once thrown away, they sit in landfills for centuries. Back in the 1940s, when plastic pens first emerged, they were a great innovation, but fast forward to today, and with 50 billion of these being made every year, they've become a significant environmental problem. And yet, nobody seemed to be talking about it.

We hear about plastic bags being banned, plastic straws being replaced with alternatives, but pens? Not a word. It seemed like an ignored problem, so I knew we had to do something about it.

The Journey to a Plastic-Free Pen

Rohit: That's really eye-opening. What were some of the insights that led you to focus on creating a completely plastic-free pen?

Saurabh: It became clear to me that the only way to truly address this problem was to eliminate plastic entirely. We started small, reducing the plastic content bit by bit. Even when we got it down to 10%, it wasn't enough for me. The difference between 0% and any amount of plastic is infinite. The goal was to make a pen that's 100% plastic-free, and I realised it was possible.

It took about four to five years of experimenting, testing different materials, and refining the design, but we eventually found a solution. Now, our pens are completely plastic-free, biodegradable, and eco-friendly. The next step was figuring out how to scale production and get these pens to market.

Innovating the Design: Challenges in Creating the Perfect Pen

Rohit: So you've eliminated plastic, but I'm sure that came with its own set of challenges. Can you tell us about the technical difficulties you faced while ensuring the pen remained functional and biodegradable?

Saurabh: Oh, there were definitely challenges! We kept the design simple and didn't change the functional part of the pen—the ink and the tip—which make up just 5% of the product. The rest, around 95%, is just plastic to hold it together. Our job was to bring that plastic content down to zero without affecting the writing experience.

Initially, we used recycled paper for the outer barrel, but the challenge was ensuring that the ink didn't seep into the paper. That's how we came up with a proprietary oil barrier, made from vegetable oil, to line the inside of the paper. It's completely biodegradable, even edible at the molecular level. Once the paper is treated and dried, the ink stays in place, and the pen performs just like any conventional one.

But getting it right took time—four years, in fact! The shelf life of the ink was another issue. At first, it dried out within 8 to 10 months. Industry standards require at least 18 months, and now, I'm happy to say we've achieved that.

Getting the Grip Right: A Matter of Ergonomics

Rohit: That's incredible! Another thing people look for in a pen is the grip. Was that a challenge too?

Saurabh: Absolutely. Ergonomics play a huge role in the success of any writing instrument. People get used to certain types of pens because of the way they feel when writing. You have your preferences, Sarjeet has his, and Shivani will have hers. We had to figure out how to cater to these different needs while staying true to our mission of being sustainable.

Right now, there are many eco-friendly pens in the market, but most are novelties. People buy them because they like the idea, but they don't use them regularly. Our goal was different—we wanted people to use our pens daily. For that to happen, the pen had to feel good in your hand, write smoothly, and be comfortable to hold. It's not enough to be eco-friendly; the pen has to be a joy to use.

Expanding the Product Range: Bamboo, Marble and Beyond

Rohit: You've also expanded into other eco-friendly products like bamboo and marble pens. What drove you to diversify your product range?

Saurabh: Yes, we realised early on that the issue wasn't just about ballpoint pens. The entire writing instrument industry—gel pens, markers, sketch pens, highlighters—needs to go plastic-free. So we began designing sustainable alternatives for all of them.

We're also exploring different materials like bamboo and even introducing products that celebrate India's rich art and craft heritage. For instance, we're launching handcrafted pens with unique designs that highlight Indian craftsmanship. It's a way for us to not only promote sustainability but also give a platform to traditional artisans.

Scaling Sustainability: The Challenge of Affordability

Rohit: Sustainability often comes at a cost, and people don't always want to pay a premium. How have you navigated the challenge of making eco-friendly products affordable?

Saurabh: This has been a major hurdle. It's true—most people aren't willing to pay a high premium for sustainable products. They might pay 10-20% more, but not three or four times the price.

What many don't realise is that the raw materials we use—like recycled paper—are often cheaper than plastic. For example, recycled paper costs around Rs. 30-35 per kg, while plastic is much more expensive. However, the process of turning that paper into a pen is where the costs come in. The plastic industry has been refining its processes for 80 years; we've had just five. But as we scale and improve the manufacturing process, I'm confident we'll bring costs down and make our products competitive with plastic pens.

We also have to think about functionality. People will buy the story of a plastic-free pen, but if it doesn't perform well, they won't come back. That's why I focus on both affordability and quality.

Nurturing the Next Generation: Educating Through Biomimicry

Rohit: You're also passionate about environmental education, especially for children. Can you share more about your initiatives in this area?

Saurabh: This is something close to my heart. I spend four to five hours every month interacting with children and introducing them to the concept of **biomimicry**—learning from nature to solve human challenges. It's something I'm personally passionate about, and I believe kids are the perfect audience for this kind of learning.

The idea is to shift the way we approach environmental education. Right now, most of it is about learning *about* nature—facts, names of trees, uses of plants, etc. But when we start learning *from* nature, that's when the magic happens. You begin to see nature as a teacher, a source of technological innovation. Just think about how trees transport water from the ground to their highest leaves. There's so much we can learn from that.

We've developed storybooks, games, and educational tools that teach kids about sustainability and biomimicry in a fun, engaging way. Kids are naturally curious, and when you give them the tools to explore, they come up with the most incredible ideas.

Key Lessons for Aspiring Eco-Entrepreneurs

Rohit: For those looking to follow in your footsteps, what advice would you give to aspiring eco-entrepreneurs?

Saurabh: I've learned a lot along the way, and there are three key lessons I'd share with anyone starting a sustainable business:

1. **Functionality First:** Sustainability is important, but if your product doesn't work well, it won't succeed. Focus on making sure it performs as well as—or better than—its conventional counterparts.

2. **Scale Matters:** Real impact comes when you can scale. Making small, handmade products might be a great start, but to change industries, you need to think about mass production and affordability.

3. **Patience and Persistence:** Nothing happens overnight. I've spent years refining our pen design, removing that last 10% of plastic. It takes time, but persistence is key.

Looking Ahead: The Future of Sustainable Innovation

Rohit: So what's next for NOTE? Where do you see the greatest opportunities for change?

Saurabh: The next few years will be about expanding our range of writing instruments—ballpoints, gel pens, highlighters—and reaching double-digit market share in the eco-friendly sector. Right now, eco-friendly products make up just 1.2% of the total market. That's abysmally low, and we need to change that.

It won't happen alone, though. We need collaboration across the entire value chain—from raw material suppliers to manufacturers and distributors. It's a collective effort, and the goal is to get there within the next 5-10 years.

Key Takeaways from Saurabh Mehta's Journey

- **Sustainability Meets Innovation:** Tackling the plastic waste problem in everyday items like pens is both a challenge and an opportunity for creative solutions.

- **Functionality is Key:** Eco-friendly products must work just as well as their conventional counterparts if they are to succeed in the market.

- **Scaling for Impact:** True change happens when sustainability goes mainstream. Scaling up production is essential for reducing costs and increasing adoption.

- **Patience and Persistence:** The path to innovation is long and filled with trial and error. Staying the course is critical to success.

- **Inspiring Future Generations:** Educating children about sustainability and encouraging curiosity through biomimicry can plant the seeds for future innovators.

Call to Action: Be Part of the Change

Saurabh's journey shows that even something as simple as a pen can contribute to a more sustainable future. Whether you're an entrepreneur looking to innovate or a consumer making conscious choices, every action counts.

Ask yourself: How can I contribute to a plastic-free future? Can I switch to more eco-friendly products? Your choices matter, and together, we can make a significant impact on the planet.

Chapter 5:

Bridging Disciplines for a Sustainable Future: Insights from Mohammed Mahmoud

When it comes to sustainability, Mohammed Mahmoud exemplifies the rare ability to blend scientific rigour with practical, real-world action. As an expert in climate adaptation, water policy, and scenario planning, he has spent his career navigating the complex interplay between environmental challenges and human needs. His journey serves as a roadmap for leaders and entrepreneurs seeking to make meaningful contributions to sustainability while balancing the demands of their industries.

Mahmoud makes it clear that solving the big challenges of our time—climate change, water scarcity, and environmental degradation—requires tearing down the walls between disciplines. It's not just about focusing on one issue, like water or energy, in isolation. Rather, it's about understanding how these challenges are deeply interconnected, requiring holistic approaches that draw on diverse perspectives.

In his early career, Mahmoud saw this firsthand. While working for a water utility in Arizona, he quickly realised that climate adaptation wasn't just a technical issue; it was a human, economic, and environmental one. Traditional approaches to water management would have focused solely on engineering solutions, but Mahmoud knew that wouldn't be enough. Instead of just talking to engineers, he brought in people from every department—legal, business, human resources—because he understood that climate change would affect every aspect of the utility's operations.

The result? A robust climate adaptation plan that was truly holistic, addressing not only water supply reliability but also the health and safety of the community, the economic viability of the utility, and the well-being of its employees. This approach reflected the complexity of sustainability challenges, which can't be tackled in silos. "Sustainability is not a solo effort," Mahmoud often reminds us, "it's a team sport that requires collaboration across disciplines."

Thinking Big and Breaking Down Barriers

Mahmoud's experience in Arizona offers a key lesson for leaders across all industries: we need to think big. Too often, businesses and organisations get trapped in narrow, discipline-specific thinking, but real innovation happens when we break down these barriers and invite different perspectives to the table. This is particularly important in sustainability, where the challenges are so complex that no single discipline can provide all the answers.

For busy professionals and young entrepreneurs, this insight is crucial. In a world where sustainability is becoming an increasingly important aspect of business strategy, the ability to collaborate across sectors is essential. Whether you're launching a start-up, scaling a business, or leading a team within a larger organisation, success will depend on your ability to integrate diverse expertise.

Take a leaf out of Mahmoud's book: invite voices from outside your immediate field to contribute to the conversation. Engineers, policymakers, financial planners, human resources professionals—all have unique insights that, when combined, can lead to more innovative and resilient solutions. In the context of climate adaptation, this interdisciplinary approach has proven to be the difference between success and failure.

The lesson here is clear: sustainability requires us to think beyond our immediate roles and responsibilities. It demands that we look at the bigger picture and bring together people from different backgrounds to craft solutions that are as comprehensive as the challenges we face.

Key Insight: Innovating for the planet means bringing diverse voices together and blending science with policy. It's about connecting the dots and ensuring solutions are as holistic as the problems they aim to solve.

Overcoming Technical Challenges: From Vision to Action

One of the most significant barriers to addressing sustainability challenges is the technical complexity of the issues involved. From climate modelling to water management, the science can be daunting, and the gap between research and practical application can feel insurmountable. This is where Mahmoud's ability to be a 'science whisperer' has made a profound impact.

Throughout his career, Mahmoud has mastered the art of translating complex scientific knowledge into practical, understandable actions that decision-makers can implement. He refers to this as being a 'science whisperer'—someone who can take highly technical information and package it in a way that policymakers and the general public can grasp. It's no small feat to distil the nuances of climate science into a format that is accessible without losing the depth and importance of the work. But as Mahmoud demonstrates, this skill is essential for driving real-world action.

While at the Middle East Institute, Mahmoud's role involved ensuring that the technical research his team produced was not just theoretically sound but also practically useful for those with the power to make decisions. His job was to simplify complex concepts, making them digestible for politicians, local leaders, and the general public. For instance, a highly detailed report on water management might be broken down into actionable, bite-sized pieces that a policymaker could use to make informed decisions.

For business leaders and entrepreneurs, Mahmoud's approach provides an important lesson: overcoming technical challenges isn't about dumbing down the content. It's about making complex information understandable and relevant to different audiences. As leaders, we need to be able to take technical or scientific issues and break them down so that everyone, from the boardroom to the street, can understand and take action. Whether you're explaining a new sustainability initiative to your team or pitching an environmentally friendly product to investors, your success will depend on your ability to communicate clearly and persuasively.

Mahmoud's work reminds us that making sustainability accessible is a crucial part of the equation. Innovation and technical expertise are vital, but they must be paired with the ability to communicate effectively if they are to be truly impactful.

Key Insight: Overcoming technical challenges means simplifying complex problems without losing their essence. Good leaders know how to make science and sustainability accessible to everyone.

Water Scarcity: Balancing Functionality and Affordability for Mass Adoption

One of the most pressing issues Mahmoud addresses in his work is water scarcity, particularly in the Middle East and North Africa (MENA) region. Climate change is exacerbating an already difficult situation, as rising temperatures and shifting rainfall patterns put additional pressure on the region's limited water resources. Yet, Mahmoud emphasises that solutions are within reach, provided they are both functional and affordable.

Take desalination, for example. This technology has become essential in regions like the Arabian Peninsula, where freshwater is scarce, and desalination plants now provide a significant portion of the region's drinking water. However, desalination isn't a one-size-fits-all solution. It is energy-intensive and costly, which means it's not always the most sustainable option in the long-term. For Mahmoud, the key to addressing water scarcity is not to rely on a single solution but to explore a mix of alternatives, including water recycling, efficiency improvements, and demand management.

Mahmoud believes that for sustainability solutions to gain widespread adoption, they need to be both scalable and affordable. It's not enough to develop innovative technologies if they remain out of reach for the communities that need them most. Desalination plants, for example, may work well in wealthy urban centres, but rural communities or low-income regions may require different, more affordable solutions. This is where innovations like water recycling programmes and community-driven efficiency initiatives can play a crucial role.

This emphasis on affordability is a key point for any business leader or policymaker. Sustainability isn't just about creating the next groundbreaking technology – it's about making sure that those innovations are accessible to the people who need them most. As Mahmoud's work shows, real impact happens when solutions are designed with functionality and affordability in mind.

For entrepreneurs, this insight is particularly relevant. While developing a cutting-edge product or service can be exciting, it's important to ask whether your innovation is scalable and whether it can reach a broad audience. Are your customers able to afford it? Will the communities that stand to benefit most have access to your solution? Balancing innovation with affordability is the key to driving mass adoption and making a real difference.

Key Insight: The real power of sustainability lies in making solutions both functional and affordable. It's not just about innovation – it's about ensuring that everyone has access to it.

Scaling Sustainable Solutions: Building Resilience Through Global Partnerships

While innovation and affordability are essential, scaling sustainable solutions requires something more—collaboration. Mohammed Mahmoud's work emphasises the importance of global partnerships in driving sustainability at scale. His experience working with governments, think tanks, and local communities across the Middle East showcases how meaningful progress happens when leaders come together to share knowledge and resources.

One of the hallmarks of Mahmoud's approach is his commitment to co-creating solutions with the communities that are directly affected by climate change. Whether it's developing water adaptation strategies in rural areas or working with local governments to implement new sustainability initiatives, Mahmoud ensures that the people on the ground are actively involved in shaping the solutions. This collaborative approach not only makes the solutions more effective but also ensures that they have the backing and support of the communities they serve.

For business leaders and entrepreneurs, Mahmoud's approach offers a valuable lesson: scaling sustainability solutions requires deep partnerships. Whether you're a CEO looking to adopt sustainable practices across your supply chain or a local government trying to implement climate policies, collaboration is key. The most successful sustainability initiatives are those that are built on strong partnerships between different sectors—businesses, governments, NGOs, and local communities.

Global collaboration is also essential for addressing the larger systemic challenges that accompany climate change. Issues like water scarcity and environmental degradation don't respect borders, which is why international cooperation is so important. Mahmoud's work in the Middle East is a testament to how partnerships that span borders and industries can drive innovation, pool resources, and create solutions that are greater than the sum of their parts.

For young entrepreneurs looking to make their mark on the sustainability landscape, global partnerships offer an opportunity to scale their innovations and expand their reach. By collaborating with partners across industries and regions, you can leverage collective expertise to tackle the complex challenges of sustainability.

Key Insight: Scaling sustainability solutions requires cross-border partnerships that are grounded in the needs of the people and communities they serve.

Patience and Persistence: The Long Game of Climate Action

If there's one thing that Mahmoud has learned in his career, it's that sustainability is not for the impatient. Change takes time, and progress often feels like it's moving at a snail's pace—especially when it comes to securing the financial commitments needed to support large-scale sustainability initiatives.

One of the biggest challenges Mahmoud faces is securing long-term financial support for sustainability projects, particularly in the global south, which includes the Middle East. He has been part of discussions at major global forums, such as COP28, where world leaders pledge to fund climate mitigation and adaptation efforts. However, as Mahmoud points out, while the promises are there, the follow-through is often slow. This has been one of the most frustrating aspects of his work, yet he remains committed to the cause.

"Patience and persistence are essential qualities for anyone working in the sustainability space," Mahmoud explains. It's easy to become disheartened when progress stalls or when financial backers hesitate to commit. But real change requires a long-term perspective. Whether you're advocating for climate finance at a global summit or trying to implement a sustainability initiative within your organisation, you need to be prepared for setbacks and delays. The key is to keep pushing forward, keep advocating, and stay committed to your goals, even when it feels like progress is slow.

This message resonates with leaders across industries. Whether you're driving a sustainability initiative within your company or working to influence government policy, it's important to remember that real change doesn't happen overnight. Achieving sustainability is a marathon, not a sprint, and leaders must be prepared for the long haul.

For entrepreneurs, especially those working in sustainability-focused ventures, Mahmoud's message is particularly relevant. Building a successful business—especially one that aims to solve complex environmental challenges—requires patience, resilience, and an unwavering commitment to your vision. There will be obstacles, but the key is to keep pushing forward, knowing that your work is contributing to a larger, long-term goal.

Key Insight: Achieving sustainability requires patience and persistence. Real change is a marathon, not a sprint, and leaders must stay committed even when progress is slow.

Mentorship and Empowerment: Fostering Leadership in Sustainability

For Mahmoud, mentorship isn't just a side project – it's central to his work. He is passionate about lifting up the next generation of sustainability leaders and ensuring that they have the opportunities and support they need to succeed. His own experiences have shaped this commitment. Early in his career, Mahmoud faced numerous roadblocks from those who were more invested in maintaining the status quo than in driving progress. But for every person who stood in his way, he found ten more who were willing to support him.

This experience taught Mahmoud the importance of being a mentor and ally to those coming up behind him. "I don't want to be the person who blocks others from making progress," he explains. Instead, he sees it as his responsibility to help the next generation overcome the obstacles he faced. Whether it's through formal mentorship programmes or simply being available to offer guidance, Mahmoud believes that today's leaders have a duty to support and empower younger voices.

For professionals and entrepreneurs, this is a powerful reminder of the importance of mentorship. As you rise in your career or build your business, consider how you can help others along the way. Mentorship isn't just about giving back—it's about fostering a culture of innovation, collaboration, and shared success. The sustainability challenges we face today will require new ideas and fresh perspectives, and the next generation of leaders will be instrumental in driving the solutions of tomorrow.

If you're in a position of leadership, think about how you can mentor and inspire the next wave of talent. Whether it's offering career advice, providing opportunities for young professionals, or simply being a sounding board for new ideas, your support can make a profound difference.

Key Insight: Empowering the next generation is essential for the long-term success of sustainability initiatives. Leaders must mentor and uplift younger voices to ensure a brighter future.

Collaboration and Industry Change: Transforming the Future of Water Management

One of the most powerful lessons from Mahmoud's work is the role of collaboration in driving industry-wide change. His experience in water management demonstrates that no single organisation or sector can tackle sustainability challenges alone. Whether it's improving water efficiency, implementing recycling programmes, or expanding desalination, the solutions to our most pressing environmental problems require strong cooperation between governments, businesses, scientists, and local communities.

Mahmoud stresses that water management in the context of climate change is one of the most urgent issues of our time. The solutions are out there, but they will only be effective if they are implemented through strong partnerships across sectors. This lesson applies not just to water management but to every industry grappling with sustainability challenges. Leaders must be willing to work together, share resources, and build strategies that are backed by both scientific research and practical application.

For business leaders, this means recognising that sustainability is not a zero-sum game. The most impactful initiatives are those that involve collaboration across industries, bringing together diverse stakeholders to develop solutions that work for everyone.

Key Insight: Collaboration is the key to transforming industries and driving sustainable change. Leaders must be willing to work across sectors and bring everyone to the table to create lasting solutions.

Conclusion: A Call to Action for Future Leaders

Mohammed Mahmoud's journey offers us a powerful blueprint for how to lead with purpose in a world facing urgent sustainability challenges. His experiences remind us that leadership in sustainability requires patience, persistence, collaboration, and mentorship. Whether you're an emerging leader or a seasoned professional, these principles are essential to driving the meaningful change our planet needs.

Now is the time for all of us to take action. Whether you're mentoring the next generation, working to scale innovative solutions, or simply finding ways to make your business more sustainable, remember that your efforts matter. Together, we can shape a more resilient, sustainable future.

A Journey into Sustainability – Karunakar Avuram's Path

Karunakar Avuram's story is one of both chance and choice—a compelling reminder that life's unexpected turns often lead us to our greatest opportunities. Initially trained as an electrical engineer, Karunakar's journey into sustainability was not a clear, predetermined path. Like many of his peers, he could have followed the booming software industry in India, but his career took a different direction when he was hired as an energy auditor. This serendipitous shift gave him a chance to apply his technical skills to something much bigger—solving global environmental challenges.

His story reflects a key truth: **sustainability leadership isn't about following a set career path—it's about finding your purpose and recognising where you can make the most impact.** We often assume that only those with a background in environmental studies or climate science can lead in sustainability, but Karunakar's engineering background gave him a unique lens to approach energy efficiency and sustainability. He applied his technical knowledge in ways that would create long-term positive change.

For example, during his time at the CII Green Business Centre, Karunakar worked extensively with the cement industry—a sector notorious for being energy-intensive. By conducting energy audits and implementing energy-saving solutions, his team helped Indian cement plants achieve world-class energy efficiency standards.

Statistics: The cement industry accounts for **8% of global CO_2 emissions**, making energy efficiency improvements in this sector critical. Karunakar's efforts, in collaboration with others, played a part in helping India's cement industry become a global leader in energy efficiency.

This chapter teaches future leaders that sustainability is not limited to specific fields; instead, it's an opportunity to apply your expertise in ways that can drive meaningful change.

Innovating for Energy Efficiency in Industry

Energy efficiency is not just about reducing consumption—it's about rethinking how industries operate at their very core. Karunakar's work across industries, particularly in the energy-heavy cement sector, underscores this point. When he and his team began conducting energy audits, they didn't just identify quick fixes; they sought **systemic changes** that would make these industries more sustainable in the long run.

Imagine this: you're tasked with auditing a large manufacturing plant, and your goal is to find energy-saving opportunities. As you walk through the facility, it's easy to get lost in the noise of machines and the complexity of processes. But Karunakar's team didn't focus solely on the obvious—they dug deep, examining not only how energy was consumed but also the **cultural resistance** that often exists in organisations. Some team members resisted change, viewing the energy audit as a fault-finding exercise.

However, the key to **overcoming resistance** is persistence. Karunakar emphasises the importance of standing by your findings when you're convinced of the data. **"We don't give up,"** he said. **"Whether they implement it or not, we show them the potential for saving energy."** This relentless pursuit of improvement reflects the mindset necessary for **innovative leadership in sustainability**.

The cement industry, with its reliance on both electrical and thermal energy, represents one of the largest sources of industrial emissions. A single cement plant can produce **up to 1 tonne of CO_2** for every tonne of cement produced. By identifying energy-saving opportunities and convincing stakeholders to adopt them, Karunakar and his team contributed to reducing that impact.

According to the International Energy Agency (IEA), energy efficiency could reduce CO_2 emissions by **40%** by 2040. Karunakar's work in the cement industry serves as a microcosm of how these broader goals can be achieved.

The Role of Audits and Data in Climate Change Mitigation

Detailed Explanation:

Data is the unsung hero of sustainability. While technology and innovation often grab the headlines, it's data that drives progress and accountability. Karunakar's work in conducting

carbon mitigation projects, including biogas, wind, and solar energy, underscores the critical role that audits and data play in achieving sustainability goals.

When we talk about **climate change mitigation**, we are talking about making decisions that lead to measurable reductions in greenhouse gas emissions. But how can we measure something as abstract as a company's carbon footprint without reliable data? This is where energy audits come into play. By rigorously assessing how energy is used and where emissions are generated, companies can create targeted strategies to reduce their environmental impact.

Karunakar was not only involved in measuring emissions but also in **making the case for renewable energy projects** by providing the financial and environmental data to support them. He worked on projects in several countries, implementing biogas, wind, and solar solutions that were not only environmentally friendly but also financially viable.

One of the most impactful projects Karunakar worked on was the implementation of biogas projects across Thailand. These projects helped the country reduce reliance on traditional fossil fuels while also reducing greenhouse gas emissions. The success of these projects was made possible by data that demonstrated both environmental benefits and a strong return on investment.

The Clean Development Mechanism (CDM) under the Kyoto Protocol, which Karunakar worked with, has supported over **8,000** projects globally, reducing emissions by an estimated **2.4 billion tonnes of CO_2 equivalent**.

Data collection and transparency are key. You can't manage what you don't measure. Leaders must prioritise using audits and data to track sustainability goals.

Implementing Sustainability at Scale – Lessons from Godrej

In the world of sustainability, **scale matters**. For sustainability to have a meaningful impact, it cannot remain confined to small-scale projects—it must be woven into the very fabric of large organisations. Karunakar's role at Godrej Consumer Products Ltd. demonstrates what it means to take sustainability to scale across a multinational corporation.

Godrej had set ambitious sustainability goals, aiming for **carbon neutrality**, **water positivity**, and **zero-waste** by 2035. Achieving these goals required systemic changes across all of its manufacturing facilities. Karunakar led the charge in implementing energy efficiency projects and renewable energy initiatives that helped Godrej reduce its environmental impact while also driving financial savings.

One of the most significant projects involved signing a renewable Power Purchase Agreement (PPA) for one of Godrej's largest facilities. This agreement allowed the plant to meet **40% of its energy needs through solar power**, reducing both carbon emissions and energy costs by **20%**.

Additionally, Godrej's commitment to sustainable packaging, driven by Karunakar's leadership, helped reduce the company's use of virgin plastics. By conducting **life cycle assessments** on its products, Godrej was able to transition to more sustainable materials, further reinforcing the company's leadership in the FMCG space.

Scaling sustainability requires setting bold, clear targets and aligning them with both operational improvements and broader environmental goals.

Social Impact through Sustainability Projects

Sustainability isn't just about reducing carbon footprints or conserving energy; it's about **creating social value**. Karunakar firmly believes that environmental and social benefits should go hand-in-hand. This chapter explores how businesses can use sustainability initiatives to foster stronger relationships with communities and improve the well-being of stakeholders.

One of the most impactful projects led by Karunakar was a **watershed management project** in Telangana, India. This project wasn't just about conserving water—it was about revitalising the local agricultural community. Farmers who had abandoned land due to water scarcity were able to return to farming thanks to the improved groundwater levels resulting from the project.

By collaborating with local communities, the watershed project didn't just benefit the environment—it created **economic opportunities** for local farmers who were able to return to agriculture and increase their livelihoods.

Similarly, in Pondicherry, Karunakar's team worked to formalise waste workers by registering them for health insurance and providing them with proper identification. These initiatives improved the workers' living conditions while addressing the growing problem of plastic waste in the community.

According to the UN, **water scarcity affects 40% of the global population**, and initiatives like watershed management can be instrumental in addressing this crisis.

Sustainability projects should create both environmental and social benefits. Leaders must focus on shared value—where business success is aligned with community prosperity.

Financial Viability of Renewable Energy Projects

One of the most persistent myths in the business world is that sustainability is expensive. Karunakar's work on renewable energy projects, including biogas, wind, and solar, demonstrates that **sustainability can be both environmentally and financially profitable**.

During his career, Karunakar worked on several **Power Purchase Agreements (PPAs)** and renewable energy projects that not only reduced carbon emissions but also saved money for the companies involved. By working with wind and solar projects, many of which were implemented under the Clean Development Mechanism (CDM), he showed that these projects could generate strong returns on investment.

One of the early wind projects Karunakar was involved with in India benefited from CDM credits, which improved the **Internal Rate of Return (IRR)**, making the project financially viable. Today, with the cost of solar energy plummeting by **89% over the last decade**, renewable energy is an even more attractive investment for companies looking to reduce their carbon footprint and their operational costs.

Leaders need to recognise that sustainability isn't just good for the planet—it's also good for the bottom line. Financial viability and environmental responsibility can and should go hand-in-hand.

Integrating ESG – A Business Imperative

In today's business environment, **Environmental, Social, and Governance (ESG)** considerations are no longer optional – they are central to long-term business success. As Karunakar pointed out, while ESG frameworks may seem like a recent trend, **leading companies** such as Tata, Godrej, and Mahindra have been integrating environmental and social concerns into their business strategies for decades.

For Karunakar, integrating ESG into business operations is not just about compliance or public relations. It's about **embedding sustainability into the core of business decision-making**. A company's ability to manage its environmental impact, improve its social footprint, and ensure ethical governance is increasingly linked to its financial performance and reputation.

At Godrej, Karunakar led the charge in achieving the company's ESG goals, including carbon neutrality, water positivity, and zero-waste to landfill. One key initiative involved **circular economy practices**, where Godrej re-engineered its packaging to minimise plastic waste and increase the use of recycled materials. This move not only reduced the company's environmental impact but also resonated with eco-conscious consumers.

According to **Deloitte**, 79% of investors globally say that ESG factors are a key part of their decision-making process. This shows a clear shift in how businesses must align their strategies with sustainability goals to attract investment.

ESG is a business imperative, not a luxury. Companies that embrace sustainability in their governance and operations are better positioned to thrive in a rapidly evolving business landscape.

Data and Digital Technologies in Sustainability

In the digital age, **data is the new currency**—and for sustainability, this couldn't be more true. The integration of digital platforms and advanced data analytics is enabling companies to **monitor, measure, and improve** their sustainability efforts more effectively than ever before. Karunakar highlights the critical role of digital technologies in managing and reporting environmental data across complex supply chains and large organisations.

Karunakar's experience at Godrej, where they transitioned from **manual Excel-based systems** to **integrated digital platforms** for monitoring their sustainability performance, underscores how digital technologies have revolutionised the way companies approach sustainability. These platforms not only made it easier to gather real-time data but also provided **predictive analytics** to help identify potential areas for improvement, thereby enabling more **data-driven decision-making**.

Karunakar implemented a **data monitoring platform** across Godrej's facilities, which allowed the company to track energy consumption, water usage, and emissions in real-time. This led to faster corrective actions, better resource allocation, and ultimately, **reduced operational costs**. The platform also sent out alerts whenever there were significant deviations in key sustainability metrics, making it easier to maintain environmental goals.

According to **Accenture**, the use of digital technologies can help companies reduce their emissions by up to **20%**, while also improving efficiency and lowering costs.

Data-driven sustainability is the future. Leaders must leverage digital platforms to track and improve sustainability metrics, ensuring that every decision is grounded in reliable and actionable data.

Shifting from Compliance to Transformation – The Future of Corporate Sustainability

While sustainability regulations and frameworks are essential, the most successful companies are those that **go beyond compliance**. Karunakar emphasises that for businesses to lead in sustainability, they must **shift from a mindset of compliance to one of transformation**. This involves integrating sustainability into every aspect of the business, from operations and supply chain management to product development and customer engagement.

Karunakar worked with Godrej to transition from traditional compliance-based sustainability reporting to an **Integrated Reporting (IR) framework**, which links financial performance with environmental and social impact. This shift allowed Godrej to move beyond simply checking regulatory boxes and instead focus on how sustainability could create long-term value for the business and its stakeholders.

This approach also extended to **supply chain management**. Recognising that their sustainability efforts would be incomplete without involving their suppliers, Godrej began working with smaller suppliers to improve their environmental performance. This initiative not only helped improve the sustainability of their supply chain but also ensured that their suppliers were aligned with their long-term sustainability goals.

A study by **Harvard Business Review** found that companies that integrate sustainability into their business model see a **20% increase in innovation** and a **16% increase in profitability**.

Sustainability is not just about meeting regulatory standards – it's about transforming how businesses operate, creating value for the environment, society, and the company itself.

Conclusion: A Future-Ready Mindset – Leading with Purpose

As we reflect on Karunakar Avuram's journey and the broader lessons from the Planecious Leaders series, it becomes clear that **sustainability leadership** is about more than implementing eco-friendly practices—it's about fostering a **mindset of resilience, innovation, and collaboration**. The leaders driving sustainability in today's business world understand that their decisions will shape the future, not just for their companies but for the planet.

Leading with purpose means recognising that business success is not just measured by profits but by the positive impact companies can have on people and the environment. Karunakar's experience in driving energy efficiency, renewable energy adoption, and sustainable business practices shows us that leadership isn't just about making incremental improvements—it's about driving **transformational change**.

The stories we've explored throughout this book illustrate that **sustainability leadership** requires:

- **Vision**: Leaders must be forward-thinking, setting bold sustainability goals that align with both their business strategy and the needs of the planet.

- **Innovation**: The willingness to embrace new technologies and approaches, such as renewable energy projects and digital data platforms, is critical for achieving sustainability at scale.

- **Collaboration**: Sustainability is not achieved in isolation. It requires partnerships with communities, governments, suppliers, and stakeholders to create a **shared value ecosystem**.

- **Patience and Persistence**: Change doesn't happen overnight. As Karunakar's journey shows, leaders must remain persistent in the face of challenges, continuously driving their sustainability agendas forward.

Call to Action:

As the next generation of business leaders, you have the opportunity—and the responsibility—to make sustainability a core part of your leadership journey. The examples in this book are a testament to what is possible when visionaries commit to creating a future where businesses operate in harmony with the environment.

Here's How You Can Start:

1. **Set bold, long-term sustainability goals** that go beyond compliance. Align these goals with your business strategy.

2. **Innovate continuously**. Embrace new technologies, explore alternative energy sources, and seek out creative ways to reduce your environmental footprint.

3. **Collaborate** with others in your industry and beyond. Together, we can drive systemic change.

4. **Never give up**. Sustainability is a journey, not a destination. Persistence and patience are key to achieving real, lasting impact.

The choices you make today will shape the world of tomorrow. Lead with purpose, innovate for the planet, and become a true champion of sustainability. The future is in your hands—make it **Future-Ready**.

Chapter 7:
Pioneers of a Sustainable Future

The world today is at a critical juncture. Climate change, environmental degradation, and dwindling natural resources present immense challenges, but they also bring unprecedented opportunities for innovation, leadership, and growth. As we move towards a greener, more sustainable future, the need for global leadership has never been greater. One country is standing out, not just in its potential but in its determination to be a guiding force in this movement. At the forefront of this transformation are leaders who understand that environmental responsibility is not just about avoiding harm, but about creating a better future—one where the economy and the environment thrive together.

In a recent conversation with Erik Solheim, a prominent global green advocate, we explored how one nation is uniquely positioned to drive the global green movement forward. Solheim, with his extensive experience as a former minister and a leader in environmental diplomacy, is deeply invested in helping countries and businesses navigate the green transition. His insights into how emerging markets can turn environmental challenges into opportunities are particularly inspiring for today's busy professionals and young entrepreneurs who are poised to lead in this space.

This conversation serves as a call to action—a reminder that sustainability is not just a policy goal but a dynamic path to innovation, job creation, and a flourishing economy. In a world where many still see environmental challenges as obstacles, Solheim offers a different perspective. He sees them as the greatest opportunities of our time.

Unleashing the Power of Renewable Energy

One of the most striking elements of the conversation was Solheim's admiration for the country's ambitious renewable energy projects. While it may seem daunting to shift from a fossil-fuel-based economy to one powered by clean energy, Solheim points out that the groundwork has already been laid. He cites a monumental solar and wind energy facility currently being developed in one of the country's arid regions, a project of such magnitude that it dwarfs the energy output of many entire nations.

This renewable energy project, which will generate 30 gigawatts when completed, is not just a testament to the country's engineering prowess, but also a symbol of its commitment to the future. "This is the kind of large-scale thinking we need," Solheim notes. "What's happening in the deserts here isn't just good for the environment; it's economically sound. It's the future of energy, and it's being led by visionaries who see the world differently."

For busy professionals and young entrepreneurs, this represents an important lesson: the path to sustainability is not just about reducing waste or cutting emissions—it's about finding opportunities for growth in the transition to green energy. The shift is already happening, and those who position themselves as leaders in this space will not only help secure a more sustainable future but will also tap into a rapidly growing market.

"Renewables like solar and wind are now the cheapest forms of energy," Solheim points out. "The old narrative that going green is expensive no longer holds true. Today, clean energy is both good for the environment and good for business." The key message here is that sustainability is no longer an option—it's an economic imperative.

The New Green Economy: Breaking the Old Paradigm

For much of modern history, economic development was tied to fossil fuels. Coal, oil, and gas powered the Industrial Revolution and were the foundation of economic growth for over a century. Nations built their infrastructure, industries, and economies on these finite resources, despite knowing their harmful effects on the environment and public health. But this dependency on fossil fuels is becoming a thing of the past.

"What we're seeing now is a fundamental shift," Solheim explains. "Renewable energy has not only caught up with fossil fuels but is surpassing them. The old model—where you had to choose between economic growth and environmental protection—is dead. Today, the two go hand-in-hand."

The significance of this shift cannot be overstated. No longer must businesses or nations choose between profitability and sustainability. In fact, choosing the green path is the smarter economic choice, offering a future where the economy grows while the planet heals. "We can increase economic prosperity, create jobs, and lift people out of poverty, all while protecting the environment," says Solheim. "That's the power of the new green economy."

For entrepreneurs, this shift presents an incredible opportunity. Those who can innovate in renewable energy, sustainable business practices, and green technology will be the business leaders of tomorrow. Whether you are developing new ways to harness solar power or creating products that reduce environmental impact, the opportunities for growth are limitless.

Leveraging Market Potential: A Strategy for Growth

One of the most exciting aspects of the country's green transformation is the size and diversity of its market. With over a billion people, the demand for sustainable products and services is immense. For entrepreneurs and business leaders, this means that if you can succeed in this market, you are well-positioned to compete globally.

"This country's market is enormous," Solheim emphasises. "If you produce something that works here, in this diverse, price-conscious market, you can sell it anywhere in the world." The country's size and complexity make it a testing ground for global competitiveness. Entrepreneurs who can navigate its varied demands will be equipped to tackle international markets with ease.

This is particularly relevant for businesses developing renewable energy solutions. As the country continues to invest in solar, wind, and other sustainable technologies, those who are at the forefront of this movement will have an edge. "Whoever makes solar panels or energy storage for this market will have a massive advantage in global markets," Solheim predicts. For busy professionals and entrepreneurs, this is a clear call to action: invest in sustainable innovation now, because the market is ready, and the world is watching.

Governance and the Role of Leadership

No transformation is possible without strong governance, and Solheim is quick to highlight the strides the country has made in this area. In the past, red tape and bureaucratic hurdles often stifled progress. But today, there is a clear push from leadership at all levels to prioritise green development. The country's leaders understand that sustainability is not just about policies; it's about creating an environment where innovation can thrive.

"There's been a real change in governance," Solheim says. "Leaders are more focused on cutting through the bureaucracy and enabling businesses to move quickly in the green space." This is particularly important for young entrepreneurs and professionals who are often deterred by administrative barriers. With a governance structure that supports innovation, there is a unique opportunity to build and scale sustainable businesses.

Leadership is not just coming from the top. Across various regions, local leaders are pushing forward ambitious green initiatives, proving that the drive for sustainability is widespread. This decentralisation of green leadership means that no matter where you are or what sector you're in, there is support for your sustainable initiatives.

The Power of Collective Action: Civil Society's Role

Another crucial factor driving the green revolution is the country's vibrant civil society. Unlike in some nations where climate scepticism can hinder progress, there is broad support for environmental initiatives from all sectors of society. This collective mindset is one of the country's greatest strengths.

"You don't see significant climate denial here," Solheim notes. "Businesses, politicians, and civil society are aligned in their belief that sustainability is the way forward." This unified approach makes it easier for businesses to pursue green initiatives without facing backlash or resistance. For young entrepreneurs and professionals, this means that there is a supportive ecosystem for sustainable innovation.

One of the most powerful elements of this civil movement is its ability to influence policy. Grassroots organisations, environmental activists, and local communities are increasingly being included in the conversation around green development. Solheim believes this is key to ensuring that the green transition is inclusive and equitable.

"It's essential that local communities benefit from green projects," Solheim says. "There needs to be a consultative process, where businesses and governments engage with communities to ensure they are part of the economic windfall." This not only fosters goodwill but also ensures that the benefits of green development are shared by all.

For business leaders, this is a reminder that sustainability is not just about technology or innovation—it's also about people. Companies that engage with local communities and ensure that their projects have a positive social impact will not only succeed but thrive.

Learning from Innovation: Scalable Solutions for the World

One of the most inspiring examples of the country's leadership in sustainability is its recent rooftop solar initiative. The plan is to install solar panels on 10 million rooftops across the country, providing clean energy to millions of households. This project is not only ambitious but also scalable, offering a model that can be replicated in other developing nations.

"This rooftop solar scheme is brilliant in its simplicity," Solheim says. "It's digital, easy to access, and shifts the financial risk away from homeowners. It's the kind of innovative thinking that can be applied in any developing nation."

For entrepreneurs, this is a clear demonstration of how scalable solutions can drive widespread change. Whether you're working on solar energy, sustainable agriculture, or eco-friendly consumer products, the goal should always be to think big—because the world is hungry for solutions that can be adapted and implemented on a global scale.

Shifting the Mindset: From Problem to Opportunity

One of the most significant cultural shifts happening in the green movement is the reimagining of environmental challenges as business opportunities. Solheim points to business leaders who are transitioning from traditional industries like coal to renewable energy, not just because it's good for the environment but because it's good for business.

"The big shift is to see climate and the environment not just as problems, but as enormous opportunities," Solheim explains. "Leaders who embrace this mindset are the ones who will drive the next wave of innovation and growth."

For entrepreneurs, this shift in perspective is critical. Instead of viewing environmental regulations or sustainability goals as burdens, they should be seen as opportunities to innovate, grow, and create new markets. The green economy is booming, and those who get ahead of the curve will be the ones leading the charge.

Advice for the Next Generation of Leaders

As the conversation draws to a close, Solheim shares his advice for young professionals and entrepreneurs who are passionate about sustainability. His message is clear: be active, stay informed, and harness the power of social media to amplify positive developments.

"Showcase the good things happening," he urges. "If you're doing something good, if you see someone else doing something good—share it. Social media is a powerful tool for spreading the message of sustainability."

He also emphasises the importance of knowledge. "Make sure you have substance," Solheim advises. "Read about climate change, understand the issues, and stay informed. Knowledge is power."

Lastly, Solheim encourages young leaders to tap into their love for the beauty of their surroundings. "Everyone knows of a beautiful place they want to protect," he says. "Whether it's a park, a beach, or a mountain, use that love of beauty to fuel your passion for sustainability."

Conclusion: The Time is Now

In a world where environmental challenges can feel overwhelming, Solheim's message is one of hope and opportunity. The green revolution is here, and it's not just about protecting the planet—it's about building a better future for all.

For today's busy professionals and young entrepreneurs, the message is clear: sustainability is the next frontier of innovation, and those who embrace it will lead the world into a prosperous, green future. The time to act is now. Whether you're developing new technologies, launching a sustainable business, or simply making greener choices in your everyday life, every action counts.

As Solheim reminds us, the path to sustainability is not just about solving problems—it's about seizing opportunities. The future is green, and it's up to all of us to shape it.

Chapter 8:
A Vision of Sustainability –
A Conversation with Dr. Aditi Mishal

In today's rapidly changing world, the pursuit of sustainability has become more than a goal—it is a necessity. The climate crisis, environmental degradation, and the depletion of natural resources are issues that no longer exist as distant threats. They are realities that affect the lives of millions today, and they pose even greater risks for future generations. For busy professionals and young entrepreneurs, the challenge is not only to be aware of these issues but to take an active role in addressing them.

In an insightful interview with Dr Aditi Mishal, a Director of Sustainability, academician, research scholar, and sustainable entrepreneur with over two decades of experience in the field, we explore what it truly means to lead with sustainability at the core. Through her groundbreaking work, innovative projects, and inspiring vision, Dr Mishal is shaping a future where sustainability is not just about environmental preservation, but a path to meaningful development, empowerment, and progress.

This chapter is a reflection on her wisdom, her journey, and a call to action for today's leaders, entrepreneurs, and changemakers to embrace sustainability as a fundamental part of their strategy for success.

The Balance Between Development and Sustainability

From the outset of the conversation, Dr Mishal dives into one of the most pressing and controversial topics in sustainability today: the perceived tension between development and sustainability. For years, the debate has centred around the belief that economic development and environmental stewardship are at odds with each other, that one must be sacrificed for the other.

"We often think that development and sustainability don't go hand-in-hand," Dr. Mishal explains. "But that's where we're wrong. True development is sustainable development. Anything else is short-sighted and will not last."

For many business leaders and entrepreneurs, the pressure to grow, scale, and increase profitability can seem to run counter to the need to protect the environment and preserve resources. But Dr. Mishal argues that sustainable development is not just possible—it is the only kind of development that will stand the test of time.

"Sustainability is not a hindrance to growth," she asserts. "In fact, it is the foundation for meaningful, long-term growth. It's about creating harmony between nature, communities, and economies."

For professionals looking to make an impact, Dr. Mishal's message is clear: sustainability is not a burden but an opportunity. By aligning business goals with environmental and social responsibility, we not only protect the planet but create value that lasts.

Awards and Responsibility: A Lifelong Commitment to Sustainability

Dr. Mishal's impressive accolades, such as the Excellence in Global Innovation Award for Outstanding Women in Global and Sustainable Development, are a testament to her lifelong dedication to this cause. But for her, these recognitions are not just milestones—they are reminders of the responsibility that comes with leadership in sustainability.

"Every award, every recognition is humbling," she says. "But more than anything, it brings a greater sense of responsibility. These awards are not just about what I've achieved; they are about what I am yet to achieve."

She recalls one of her earliest memories of receiving an award as a child, a moment that sparked her drive to do more and be better. This motivation has only grown stronger with each recognition. As a leader in sustainability, she feels a deep responsibility to use her platform to inspire others, guide corporate and institutional efforts, and stay true to the principles of sustainable development.

For entrepreneurs and business leaders, this sense of responsibility is something Dr. Mishal encourages. Recognition, whether it comes in the form of awards, profits, or market success, should always come with a commitment to give back—especially when it comes to the environment.

"The more we achieve, the more we owe to the world around us," she emphasises. "Sustainability isn't just a job—it's a purpose. It's a responsibility we carry into every aspect of our work and lives."

The Smart Toilet Tracking System: Innovation for Social Impact

One of Dr Mishal's most impactful projects is the Smart Toilet Tracking System, a technology-driven initiative designed to ensure the proper use and maintenance of public sanitation facilities. This project was born out of the larger national campaign to make open defecation-free areas by providing accessible toilets to households across the country. However, the reality she observed was that many of these toilets were either not used or repurposed as storage spaces due to a lack of water or poor infrastructure.

"The problem wasn't just about building toilets – it was about ensuring they were used for their intended purpose," Dr. Mishal explains. "That's where technology comes in."

Dr. Mishal worked with students to develop a system that monitors the usage of public toilets to ensure that they are functional and serving the communities they were built for. This initiative not only addresses a crucial public health issue but also demonstrates how technology and sustainability can work together to solve real-world problems.

"Technology often gets a bad reputation when it comes to sustainability," Dr. Mishal acknowledges. "But I've always believed that technology can empower and enable sustainable development. It's all about how we use it."

This project is a powerful example of how innovative thinking and a systems approach can tackle complex challenges. For entrepreneurs, the lesson here is to look beyond the obvious solutions and dig deeper into the systems that create the problems in the first place. By using technology and design thinking, you can create solutions that are scalable, impactful, and sustainable.

Youth Leadership: Engaging the Next Generation

Dr Mishal has worked closely with young people throughout her career, and she believes that the next generation is uniquely positioned to lead the charge on sustainability. She points out that today's youth have grown up in a world where climate change, deforestation, water scarcity, and waste management are pressing concerns. Unlike previous generations, they are more aware of these challenges and more eager to contribute to solutions.

"What I've seen in young people is a genuine desire to make a difference," she says. "They don't just want to talk about sustainability - they want to take action."

Dr Mishal shares an inspiring story about her work with students from MIT's Media Lab on a project during the Kumbh Mela, a large religious festival that brings millions of people to the banks of a river for worship. Sanitation is a significant issue during the event, and the project she worked on with students aimed to address this by introducing biodigester toilets in collaboration with a defence organisation.

"The students were so committed," she recalls. "They didn't just design the project – they were involved in every step, from getting funding to overseeing the installation of the toilets. It was their passion and drive that made the project a success."

This experience reinforced Dr. Mishal's belief that young people are not only the future of sustainability—they are the present. For professionals and entrepreneurs, her message is clear: engage with youth, empower them to take leadership roles, and collaborate with them to bring innovative solutions to life.

Sustainability and Spirituality: The Wisdom of the Bhagavad Gita

For Dr Mishal, sustainability is not just a practical or economic concern—it is also deeply rooted in spirituality. She draws inspiration from the Bhagavad Gita, a spiritual text that she believes holds the key to understanding the true meaning of sustainability.

"My spiritual father always taught me that inner sustainability leads to outer sustainability," she shares. "If we want to create a sustainable world, we first have to cultivate sustainability within ourselves."

According to Dr Mishal, much of the environmental degradation we see today is a result of greed and exploitation—the belief that the Earth and its resources exist solely for human enjoyment. But the Bhagavad Gita offers a different perspective: we are caretakers of the planet, entrusted with its resources to ensure the flourishing of all life, not just our own.

"The five elements—earth, water, fire, air, and space—don't belong to us," she says. "They are gifts that we have a responsibility to care for. Sustainability starts with understanding this stewardship."

For entrepreneurs, this message is particularly powerful. In a world driven by profits and consumption, it's easy to lose sight of the bigger picture. But Dr. Mishal encourages business leaders to adopt a mindset of stewardship—one where success is measured not only by financial gain but by the positive impact on the environment and society.

The Role of Technology in Advancing Sustainability

Technology plays a critical role in advancing sustainable practices, and Dr. Mishal is a strong advocate for integrating innovation with sustainability. In her work, she has seen firsthand how technological advancements—from simple machines to complex systems—can improve lives and protect the environment.

"When we talk about technology, it's not just about IT systems," she explains. "It's about creating innovative, sustainable technologies that solve real-world problems."

Dr Mishal highlights the importance of co-creating technology with the communities who will use it. This approach ensures that the solutions are practical, effective, and sustainable. For example, she mentions the development of machines that reduce the physical burden on sanitation workers and measure harmful gas concentrations to protect their health.

But technology is not just about gadgets and machines—it's also about processes and systems. Dr. Mishal emphasises the importance of adopting a circular economy approach, where resources are used efficiently, and waste is minimised. This way of thinking ensures that products and technologies are designed with their entire lifecycle in mind, from production to disposal.

For entrepreneurs, this presents a huge opportunity. By embracing sustainable technologies and innovative business models, you can create products and services that not only meet market demand but also contribute to a more sustainable world.

ESG: A Game-Changer for Corporate Responsibility

Dr. Mishal believes that Environmental, Social, and Governance (ESG) principles are set to be a game-changer in the corporate world. As businesses start to recognise their responsibility towards sustainable development, ESG frameworks provide a roadmap for integrating sustainability into corporate strategies.

"When companies realise that they are responsible for more than just profits, they start to take sustainability seriously," she says. "This is where ESG comes in."

Dr Mishal highlights examples of companies that are leading the way in sustainable fashion, green buildings, and ethical production. These businesses are proving that sustainability is not just a trend – it's the future of responsible business.

For professionals in the corporate world, ESG represents an opportunity to align business goals with sustainability. By adopting ESG principles, companies can create value that goes beyond financial performance and contributes to the well-being of society and the environment.

Advice for Sustainability Enthusiasts

As the interview comes to a close, Dr Mishal offers valuable advice for those passionate about sustainability. She emphasises the importance of resilience and persistence, especially when faced with seemingly insurmountable challenges.

"These challenges are like mountains," she says. "But every time we push against them, we become stronger."

She encourages sustainability enthusiasts to work smarter, not just harder. This means finding innovative solutions, collaborating with key stakeholders, and positioning yourself in places of influence where you can make a real difference.

For entrepreneurs and business leaders, her final message is clear: don't just work for success—work for significance. Sustainable development is not just a profession; it's a calling to create a better, more equitable world for future generations.

A Call to Action: Be the Change

In a world where environmental challenges are growing by the day, Dr. Mishal's words are a powerful reminder that each of us has a role to play in creating a sustainable future.

Whether you're an entrepreneur, a corporate leader, or a young professional, the time to act is now.

"Sustainable development is not just a goal—it's our purpose," Dr. Mishal says. "We are here to make a difference, to leave the world better than we found it."

For those ready to take up this challenge, the path forward is clear: embrace sustainability in your work, your business, and your life. Be the change that leads the world towards a future where development and sustainability go hand-in-hand.

Chapter 9:

Empowering Communities and Building a Sustainable Future – The Vision of Ankur Vaidya

How Grassroots Leadership, Cultural Wisdom and Strategic Action Drive Sustainable Development

In today's world, sustainability has moved from being a choice to a necessity. Forward-thinking leaders are inspiring communities to take action, and one such leader is Ankur Vaidya, Chairman of the Federation of Indian Associations (FIA), the largest and oldest grassroots non-profit umbrella organisation on the East Coast of the United States. His work focuses on empowering the Indian American diaspora while integrating sustainability into community initiatives. Ankur's leadership blends tradition with modern solutions, creating a roadmap for professionals and entrepreneurs alike to drive long-term, impactful change.

This chapter explores his approach to sustainability and how it can serve as an inspiration for others. Through examples and practical insights, readers will gain a better understanding of how community involvement, cultural preservation, and strategic action can lead to a more sustainable future.

Driving Awareness: Building a Cognizant and Engaged Community

Key Takeaway: Fostering sustainability begins with awareness, and effective community engagement can set the foundation for long-term sustainable development.

A key challenge faced by many communities is a lack of awareness when it comes to sustainable development. As the Chairman of FIA, Ankur Vaidya is deeply involved in creating platforms that raise awareness about sustainability within the Indian American community. While a significant portion of the community is aware of the importance of sustainability, there is still a lot of work to be done in broadening this understanding.

"Awareness has to start at the ground level," he explains. "Whether it's about reducing food waste or encouraging the use of refillable water bottles, small actions can make a huge difference."

To promote this, FIA organised a gala in New York focusing on the concept of Zero Food Waste. This event, attended by influential community members, aimed to show how simple yet impactful changes could drastically reduce food waste and promote sustainability. The positive reception proved that communities are open to change when given the right platforms and information.

The lesson here for professionals and entrepreneurs is that raising awareness is the first step to driving sustainable development. Whether through localised events or broader awareness campaigns, educating the community is essential to get people engaged in sustainability efforts.

Engaging the Youth: Mobilising the Next Generation for Sustainable Development

Key Takeaway: Empowering the youth to lead sustainable efforts creates long-term societal change, but they must be engaged through relatable, actionable initiatives.

The younger generation plays a critical role in shaping the future of sustainability. Their openness to new ideas and eagerness to embrace change make them natural advocates for sustainable practices. Engaging the youth, however, requires strategies that align with their interests and daily habits.

"From electric cars to ride-sharing services, young people are already embracing sustainable practices. There's ongoing debate about the environmental impact of electric cars, but what's important is the shift in mindset towards cleaner alternatives. Additionally, simple habits like prolonging the life of electronics—using a phone for several years instead of upgrading annually can significantly reduce electronic waste," he points out. Schools are also playing a key role in these efforts, encouraging students to bring refillable water bottles instead of using plastic. This shift towards reusable items is becoming the norm, and the message is being spread effectively through education systems.

The takeaway here is that engaging the youth means embedding sustainability into their daily lives. For entrepreneurs and business leaders, creating sustainable solutions that fit seamlessly into the habits of younger generations is key to building long-term change.

Leadership from the Top: The Power of Influence in Sustainable Movements

Key Takeaway: Sustainable change is most effectively driven from the top, with leaders and influencers setting trends that trickle down to grassroots communities.

While grassroots movements are important, Ankur Vaidya emphasises that real change often starts at the top. In today's world, celebrities, political figures, and influencers have the power to set trends that can quickly gain traction within communities. When top-level leaders embrace sustainability, the message spreads more effectively and creates faster adoption among the general population.

"It's challenging to build momentum from the grassroots alone," he says. "But when a high-profile figure endorses sustainable practices, the community is more likely to follow suit."

This idea is not only applicable to large-scale celebrities but also to business and community leaders. By modelling sustainable behaviour, they can set the example for others. When influencers adopt sustainable habits, such as reducing their carbon footprint or promoting eco-friendly products, the community is more likely to follow.

For professionals and entrepreneurs, the lesson is to leverage top-down influence when implementing sustainable initiatives. Whether through partnerships with influencers or encouraging leadership to set an example, this approach can create a ripple effect, inspiring more people to adopt sustainable behaviours.

Cultural Integration: Blending Tradition with Modern Sustainability

Key Takeaway: Sustainable development can be more impactful when traditional cultural practices are integrated, but they must be adapted to meet modern standards of hygiene and safety.

Culture plays a significant role in shaping community behaviours, and traditional practices can serve as valuable tools in sustainable development. Mr Vaidya believes that many of the sustainable techniques used in Indian culture for centuries—such as clay utensils or plates made from leaves—can still offer solutions for today's environmental challenges. However, these practices must be adapted to modern hygiene and safety standards.

"For sustainable practices rooted in our cultural heritage to be accepted today, there needs to be a balance between tradition and modern hygiene," he says. "Take the example of disposable plates made from leaves. They're environmentally friendly, but hygiene concerns often prevent them from being widely used."

A modern example of cultural practices gaining global traction is the use of the 'Namaste' gesture during the COVID-19 pandemic. A hands-free greeting, deeply rooted in Indian tradition, it became a globally accepted practice because it fit the need for hygiene during the pandemic. This demonstrates that cultural practices can be adapted to modern contexts, offering sustainable and practical solutions.

For entrepreneurs and business leaders, the takeaway is to innovate by blending tradition with modern requirements. By doing so, cultural practices can be preserved while contributing to sustainability in a meaningful way.

Inclusivity in Sustainability: Ensuring No One Is Left Behind

Key Takeaway: Sustainable development efforts must be inclusive and designed to benefit all communities, regardless of socio-economic status.

One of the essential principles of sustainable development is that it must benefit everyone. Mr Vaidya highlights that sustainability should not be seen as something exclusive to affluent communities. Rather, it's a broad concept with benefits for all, particularly underrepresented or marginalised groups.

"Sustainability applies to everyone," he says. "From urban elites to rural communities, the benefits of reducing pollution and promoting eco-friendly practices are universal."

An example is how many rural communities in India still use clay utensils, which are not only sustainable but also have health benefits. These traditional practices show that sustainability is not new; it has been part of daily life for generations. However, inclusivity ensures that these practices reach everyone and that sustainable development benefits people from all walks of life.

For entrepreneurs and professionals, the key takeaway is to ensure that sustainability efforts are inclusive. Whether it's through making eco-friendly products more affordable or ensuring that sustainability programmes reach underrepresented communities, inclusivity should be at the heart of every sustainability initiative.

Grassroots Movements: Mobilising Community-Level Action for Sustainable Impact

Key Takeaway: While leadership from the top is crucial, grassroots movements remain essential for driving localised, community-level sustainability initiatives.

Although top-down influence can create a wider reach, grassroots movements are still critical for creating localised change. Communities often have the power to drive small-scale initiatives that build up over time, creating a larger impact. This is where grassroots actions like reducing waste at community events or encouraging families to adopt sustainable habits come into play.

The Zero Food Waste initiative, which was promoted by FIA at a community-level, is an example of how grassroots efforts can spark meaningful change. The initiative encouraged individuals to reduce food waste at events, showing them how simple changes could make a significant environmental difference.

"True change happens when people start adopting sustainable practices in their daily lives," Mr. Vaidya said. "It starts small, with actions like reducing waste, but those actions grow into broader, more impactful movements."

For professionals and entrepreneurs, the key takeaway is to balance top-down influence with grassroots efforts. By creating programmes that engage people at the community-level, leaders can foster small but meaningful changes that lead to long-term impact.

Conclusion: A Call to Action for Future Leaders

Ankur Vaidya's leadership at the FIA and his approach to sustainable development reflect a deep understanding of community dynamics and cultural preservation. He has successfully demonstrated how awareness, youth engagement, cultural integration, and top-down leadership can all work together to drive meaningful change.

For busy professionals and young entrepreneurs, Ankur's insights offer a roadmap for building sustainable, resilient communities and businesses. Whether it's through leveraging cultural practices, mobilising the youth, or using influential voices to promote sustainability, the path to a more sustainable future is clear. It requires innovation, inclusivity, and a long-term vision.

As we face global challenges, the call to action is simple: lead with purpose, inspire others, and embrace sustainability as a core part of your strategy. The future depends on the actions we take today. Now is the time to act.

Chapter 10:
The Role of MSMEs in Driving Sustainable Growth

Introduction: The Backbone of Economic Progress

Micro, Small, and Medium Enterprises (MSMEs) are often described as the backbone of developing economies. In India, MSMEs account for **30% of the country's GDP** and contribute to **45% of the nation's exports**. They are the driving force behind industrial production, rural development, and employment generation, particularly in the semi-urban and rural sectors. For a nation like India, where inclusive growth is a critical objective, MSMEs play a central role in bridging the gap between the local economy and the global market.

Yet, as we march towards an increasingly digital and globalised economy, the expectations on businesses have changed. Today, MSMEs are not just valued for their role in economic development; they are also seen as key players in the fight against climate change. But here's the exciting part—*this shift doesn't just come with challenges; it opens up new opportunities* for MSMEs to grow, diversify, and build resilience while contributing to a more sustainable world.

The question for every business leader becomes: How can we contribute to sustainability while ensuring long-term profitability? And, perhaps more importantly, *how can sustainability become the catalyst for growth* rather than a hindrance?

Understanding the MSME Landscape: Challenges and Potential

The MSME sector is diverse, covering industries from textiles to agriculture to technology. Each of these sectors faces its own unique set of challenges, but the unifying factor across the board is the scale at which MSMEs operate. With limited financial resources, many MSMEs are reluctant to invest in long-term sustainability projects, fearing they may not have the immediate returns needed to justify the investment.

However, this mindset is rapidly shifting. With growing awareness and incentives around sustainability, businesses are realising that *investing in green technologies and practices is not just good for the planet—it's good for business.*

Let's take a closer look at the challenges MSMEs face in integrating sustainable practices and how these challenges can be turned into opportunities for growth.

1. Limited Access to Capital

One of the primary challenges MSMEs face is limited access to capital. Many small businesses operate on tight margins, which makes it difficult to invest in new technologies or adopt more efficient, sustainable processes. But here's the interesting part—*the landscape is changing*. Financial institutions and governments are increasingly offering incentives for businesses that demonstrate a commitment to sustainability. Whether through green bonds, government grants, or reduced tax rates, businesses that can prove their sustainable practices often find it easier to secure funding.

In fact, India has begun to introduce **green financing initiatives** that directly support MSMEs in their sustainability journeys. These programmes provide businesses with the capital needed to invest in energy-efficient machinery, renewable energy, and cleaner production methods.

For example, switching from conventional energy sources to renewable alternatives like solar or wind can drastically reduce operational costs over time. The initial investment may seem daunting, but with the help of green financing, MSMEs can offset these costs while generating long-term savings.

2. Knowledge Gaps and Lack of Awareness

Another hurdle for MSMEs is the knowledge gap. Many businesses are simply unaware of the benefits that sustainability can bring, or they don't know where to start when it comes to integrating green practices into their operations. This lack of awareness can prevent MSMEs from making the necessary investments in sustainability.

However, **education and awareness programmes** are beginning to change this narrative. Several initiatives have been launched to help MSMEs understand how they can adopt sustainable practices while remaining profitable. These programmes focus on creating awareness about renewable energy, energy efficiency, water conservation, and waste management, among other topics.

Governments, non-governmental organisations (NGOs), and private institutions are increasingly collaborating to provide MSMEs with the tools, training, and resources needed to thrive in a greener economy. As businesses become more informed about the benefits of sustainability, they are better equipped to make decisions that will positively impact both their profitability and the environment.

3. Regulatory Pressure

The third challenge is navigating the regulatory landscape. As the world shifts towards a more sustainable future, governments are tightening environmental regulations. From stricter emissions standards to mandates on waste management, businesses will need to comply with these regulations or risk penalties.

But there's a silver lining: **regulatory pressure can also drive innovation**. Businesses that anticipate these regulations and proactively adopt sustainable practices will be in a better position to compete. In fact, those who embrace sustainability early can transform regulatory compliance from a burden into a competitive advantage.

By adopting green practices now, MSMEs can stay ahead of the regulatory curve, gaining the trust of both consumers and governments alike. In doing so, they not only protect themselves from future penalties but also position themselves as industry leaders in sustainability.

Sustainability: A Global Business Imperative

As global attention shifts towards environmental issues, sustainability is no longer just an option—it's a necessity. The effects of climate change, such as erratic weather patterns, rising sea levels, and biodiversity loss, are becoming more apparent every year. Governments, businesses, and consumers are demanding solutions, and MSMEs have a critical role to play.

But here's the exciting part: MSMEs don't have to choose between profitability and sustainability. In fact, businesses that embrace green practices are often more resilient, more competitive, and more attractive to investors.

1. Gaining a Competitive Edge

In a world where consumers increasingly prioritise sustainability, MSMEs that adopt environmentally friendly practices can stand out in a crowded market. A commitment to sustainability can set your business apart, giving you a **competitive edge** over businesses that have yet to go green. This is particularly important as more and more global corporations are aligning themselves with suppliers that can help them meet their own sustainability goals.

Think about the fashion industry, where sustainable brands are growing rapidly due to increasing demand from environmentally conscious consumers. MSMEs in textiles, for example, can gain a foothold in new markets by adopting sustainable sourcing, energy-efficient production methods, and waste reduction practices. This is not just about doing the right thing; it's about staying relevant in a rapidly changing marketplace.

2. Attracting Investment

The link between sustainability and investment is becoming stronger. Investors are increasingly drawn to businesses that prioritise environmental, social, and governance (ESG) criteria. Why? Because **sustainable businesses are often seen as lower-risk, long-term investments**. Investors know that companies focusing on sustainability are better equipped to navigate future challenges, such as stricter regulations or changing consumer preferences.

For MSMEs, this means that demonstrating a commitment to sustainability can open doors to new funding opportunities. By positioning yourself as a responsible business, you attract the attention of investors who are eager to support companies making a positive impact.

3. Building Resilience

Sustainability is not just about being environmentally friendly – it's about building resilience into your business model. By reducing your reliance on non-renewable resources, investing in energy-efficient technologies, and improving your waste management processes, you're creating a business that's better prepared for the future.

For example, a company that relies on fossil fuels for energy is vulnerable to price fluctuations and supply chain disruptions. On the other hand, an MSME that invests in renewable energy solutions, like solar or wind, is insulated from these risks. By making your operations more sustainable, you're not only protecting the environment but also safeguarding your business from external shocks.

Sustainability in Action: Practical Steps for MSMEs

Now that we understand why sustainability matters, let's get practical. What can MSMEs do today to start their sustainability journey? Here are some actionable steps that can help businesses integrate sustainability into their operations while maintaining profitability.

1. Start Small but Think Big

Sustainability doesn't have to be an all-or-nothing proposition. You don't need to overhaul your entire business overnight to make a positive impact. Start by identifying small, manageable changes that can reduce your environmental footprint. This could be as simple as switching to energy-efficient lighting, implementing water-saving measures, or reducing waste in your production process.

Over time, these small changes can add up to significant environmental and financial benefits. Once you've made these initial improvements, you can start to think bigger. For example, you might consider transitioning to renewable energy sources or investing in new, more efficient equipment.

2. Collaborate with Other Businesses

Sustainability is often more achievable when businesses work together. MSMEs can collaborate with other companies, industry groups, or even NGOs to share resources, knowledge, and best practices. These collaborations can help reduce costs and increase the impact of sustainability initiatives.

For example, MSMEs in the same industry can work together to develop shared supply chains that prioritise sustainability. By pooling their resources, they can negotiate better prices for sustainable materials or invest in shared renewable energy projects. These collaborations not only reduce costs but also help businesses achieve their sustainability goals more quickly.

3. Leverage Government Incentives

Governments around the world are offering a range of incentives to encourage businesses to adopt sustainable practices. These incentives might include tax breaks, grants, or low-interest loans for businesses that invest in renewable energy, energy efficiency, or waste reduction.

MSMEs should take full advantage of these incentives to offset the costs of implementing sustainable practices. By doing so, they can make sustainability a more financially viable option while also reducing their environmental impact.

4. Measure and Monitor Progress

One of the most important aspects of integrating sustainability into your business is measuring and monitoring your progress. Set clear goals for reducing your carbon footprint, conserving water, or cutting waste, and track your performance over time. This not only helps ensure that you're making progress but also provides a powerful tool for communicating your sustainability efforts to customers, investors, and partners.

By showcasing your commitment to sustainability, you can strengthen your brand reputation and attract more business.

Call to Action: The Time for Change is Now

The time for MSMEs to embrace sustainability is now. The global economy is shifting, and businesses that fail to adapt risk being left behind. But for those that do embrace sustainability, the opportunities are endless.

By integrating green practices into your operations, you not only reduce your environmental impact but also improve your competitiveness, attract investment, and build a more resilient business. Sustainability is not just a trend – it's the future of business.

So, start today. Take the first steps towards sustainability by making small changes in your operations, collaborating with others, and leveraging government incentives. The benefits are clear: a more profitable, resilient, and sustainable business that's ready for the challenges of tomorrow.

Chapter 11

Navigating the Carbon Credit Market for MSMEs

Understanding Carbon Credits: A New Business Frontier

In today's evolving business landscape, sustainability isn't just a buzzword—it's an opportunity for growth. For Micro, Small, and Medium Enterprises (MSMEs), carbon credits offer a pathway to align with global sustainability goals while unlocking new revenue streams. A carbon credit represents one tonne of carbon dioxide (or its equivalent in other greenhouse gases) that your business has reduced or removed from the atmosphere. It's not just an environmental victory—it's a financial opportunity.

Here's the exciting part: those credits can be sold or traded, giving your business a financial incentive to reduce its emissions. MSMEs are often more agile than large corporations, making them ideally positioned to adopt sustainable practices quickly and reap the rewards. Imagine reducing your emissions and getting paid for it—carbon credits make that possible.

So, what does this mean for your MSME? Simply put, sustainability is no longer a luxury; it's a strategic advantage. By participating in the carbon credit market, you can boost your profitability while contributing to global climate goals. This isn't just about compliance; it's about seizing a new business opportunity in a world that increasingly rewards environmentally conscious companies.

How Carbon Markets Work

Let's break down how carbon markets function. Think of them as platforms where businesses trade emissions reductions. The two primary markets are *compliance markets* and *voluntary markets*, and both offer opportunities for MSMEs to capitalise on sustainability efforts.

Compliance Markets: The Regulated Approach

In compliance markets, governments regulate the emissions of large industries like energy, transportation, and heavy manufacturing. Companies in these sectors must keep their emissions within a legally mandated limit. If they exceed this cap, they are required to buy carbon credits from businesses that have successfully reduced their emissions.

This is where MSMEs can play a role. By reducing emissions, your business can earn carbon credits that larger corporations in compliance markets need to purchase. Essentially, you're helping them meet their legal obligations while generating income for your business.

Voluntary Markets: The Freedom to Offset

Voluntary carbon markets are where businesses choose to reduce or offset their emissions, even when not required by law. These markets are driven by companies that want to showcase their commitment to sustainability. Whether it's a multinational aiming for carbon neutrality or a company catering to eco-conscious customers, these businesses buy carbon credits to offset the emissions they can't directly eliminate.

For MSMEs, this is an exciting space. Imagine you've adopted renewable energy in your operations, reducing your emissions significantly. By earning carbon credits, you can sell them in the voluntary market to companies eager to enhance their sustainability profile. This positions your MSME not only as a green leader but also as a valuable partner in the supply chain of environmentally responsible corporations.

Opportunities for MSMEs in Carbon Markets

Now, let's explore how MSMEs can directly benefit from participating in the carbon credit market. The opportunities go far beyond just environmental compliance — they offer significant financial and branding advantages as well.

1. Economic Opportunities: Sustainability as a Revenue Stream

For many MSMEs, transitioning to greener practices can feel daunting. But the truth is, carbon credits transform sustainability into a revenue-generating opportunity. By reducing emissions, your business can generate credits that you can sell. This extra income can help you invest further in sustainable technologies or expand your operations.

Picture this: you install solar panels at your facility. Not only do you cut energy costs, but you also reduce emissions and earn carbon credits. You then sell those credits in the carbon market, turning your investment into a new revenue stream. This kind of strategic thinking turns sustainability into a long-term financial benefit for your business.

2. Enhancing Brand Reputation: The Green Advantage

In today's marketplace, consumers and clients are increasingly prioritising sustainability. By integrating carbon credits into your business model, you demonstrate that your MSME is serious about environmental responsibility. This can significantly enhance your brand reputation, especially when vying for contracts with larger corporations that have sustainability commitments.

Imagine competing for a supply contract with a major retailer. By showcasing your carbon reduction efforts and the credits you've earned, you immediately differentiate your business from competitors. Companies are more likely to choose partners who align with their sustainability goals, which means your commitment to reducing emissions could directly translate into winning new business.

3. Regulatory Compliance and Future-Proofing

Governments worldwide are tightening regulations around emissions, and it's only a matter of time before stricter laws impact MSMEs across industries. By participating in carbon markets now, you prepare your business for future regulations. Staying ahead of compliance helps you avoid costly fines and ensures you're well-positioned as regulations evolve.

Think of this as a proactive strategy. Rather than scrambling to meet new standards down the road, you can start reducing your carbon footprint today, earning credits and positioning your business as an industry leader in sustainability. This foresight will pay dividends as the global economy increasingly favours green businesses.

4. Access to Funding and Investment Opportunities

Sustainability is no longer optional for attracting investment. Investors and financial institutions are actively seeking businesses that prioritise environmental, social, and governance (ESG) criteria. By demonstrating your commitment to reducing emissions and participating in carbon credit markets, you make your MSME more attractive to investors.

Let's say you're looking to expand your business and need additional capital. By showcasing your sustainability initiatives, carbon credits earned, and commitment to ESG principles, you present a compelling case to potential investors. Sustainability is now a critical factor in investment decisions, and MSMEs that adopt green practices are more likely to secure funding.

Key Sectors for Carbon Credits

While carbon credits can benefit businesses in nearly every sector, certain industries stand out for their potential to reduce emissions and generate substantial credits. Let's explore three key sectors where MSMEs can make the most impact.

1. Renewable Energy: Generating Clean Power

Renewable energy is one of the most effective ways to reduce carbon emissions. For MSMEs, switching to renewable energy sources—such as solar or wind power—can significantly cut emissions and generate carbon credits. The financial benefits are twofold: you reduce your energy costs while earning credits that can be sold in the market.

Imagine you own a small factory and decide to install solar panels on the roof. Not only do you slash your electricity bills, but you also reduce your reliance on fossil fuels. This reduction in emissions earns you carbon credits, which you can sell to companies looking to offset their carbon footprint. Over time, this strategy both boosts your bottom line and enhances your brand as a green leader.

2. Agriculture and Forestry: Nature's Carbon Sinks

Agriculture and forestry are uniquely positioned to benefit from carbon credits. These sectors offer opportunities to sequester carbon—through tree planting, organic farming, or improving soil health. For MSMEs involved in these industries, sustainable practices can generate credits while preserving natural ecosystems.

Let's say your MSME is in the agriculture sector. By switching to organic farming methods or engaging in agroforestry (planting trees alongside crops), you help sequester carbon from the atmosphere. This earns you carbon credits while enhancing the sustainability of your operations. Not only are you improving your farm's resilience, but you're also turning green practices into profits.

3. Textiles and Manufacturing: Reducing Emissions, Increasing Profits

Textile manufacturing is an energy-intensive industry, making it a prime candidate for carbon reduction efforts. MSMEs in this sector can significantly reduce their carbon footprint by adopting energy-efficient technologies, reducing waste, or using sustainable raw materials. Each of these actions generates carbon credits, which can be sold in the market.

Consider a textile MSME that upgrades its machinery to energy-efficient models, cutting energy consumption and emissions. By reducing emissions, the company earns carbon credits, which it can sell to larger corporations looking to offset their own environmental impact. Over time, this leads to lower operational costs, increased revenue from carbon credits, and a stronger position in the market.

Case Study: A Practical Example of Success

Let's put this all together with a real-world example. Imagine a textile MSME based in India that produces fabrics for export. Like many businesses in the textile industry, this MSME faces growing pressure from international clients to reduce its environmental impact.

The business begins by installing solar panels, reducing its reliance on grid electricity and cutting its carbon emissions by 40%. Next, it invests in energy-efficient machinery, reducing its overall energy consumption by another 20%. These combined efforts significantly reduce the company's carbon footprint, allowing it to generate carbon credits.

The MSME then sells these credits in the voluntary market, creating a new revenue stream that helps offset the initial investment in solar panels and energy-efficient equipment. But the benefits don't stop there. By demonstrating its commitment to sustainability, the MSME secures a long-term contract with a major European retailer that values green practices. This contract not only increases the company's revenue but also positions it as a leader in sustainable textile production.

This case study illustrates how carbon credits can turn sustainability into a competitive advantage, helping businesses grow while reducing their environmental impact.

Strategies for Success

So, how can your MSME tap into the carbon credit market and turn sustainability into a profitable business strategy? Here are four essential strategies:

1. Conduct a Carbon Footprint Assessment

Start by understanding where your emissions are coming from. Conducting a carbon footprint assessment allows you to identify the areas where you can make the most significant reductions. Various tools and consultants can help you measure your emissions accurately and set achievable reduction targets.

2. Invest in Sustainable Technologies

Reducing emissions requires investment, but the payoff is substantial. Whether it's switching to renewable energy, upgrading to energy-efficient machinery, or improving waste management, each step you take will reduce your emissions and earn you carbon credits. These investments will also reduce your operating costs over time.

3. Engage with Carbon Markets

Once you've reduced your emissions, it's time to participate in carbon markets. Whether you're trading in compliance or voluntary markets, there are opportunities to sell your carbon credits for a profit. Work with experts who can guide you through the process, ensuring that you maximise the value of your credits.

4. Build Long-Term Partnerships

Sustainability is a growing priority for large corporations, and MSMEs that demonstrate their commitment to reducing emissions will find themselves in high demand. Build long-term partnerships with companies that value sustainability and position your business as a key player in the green economy.

Call to Action

The carbon credit market offers MSMEs a unique opportunity to grow sustainably while generating new revenue streams. By reducing emissions, earning carbon credits, and participating in carbon markets, you can position your business as a leader in the global transition to a low-carbon economy.

Now is the time to act. Start by assessing your carbon footprint, exploring how your business can reduce emissions, and diving into the world of carbon credits. The future of business is green—and MSMEs have the agility, innovation, and drive to lead the way.

Chapter 12:

Building a Sustainable Future: Lessons from Leading Experts

Introduction: Sustainability as a Strategic Business Imperative

In today's world, sustainability is no longer a side initiative or a feel-good corporate programme. It's a strategic imperative. Businesses, whether large corporations or MSMEs, are realising that their long-term viability is inextricably linked to the health of the environment and the global community. The conversation has shifted from "Should we focus on sustainability?" to "*How* can we make sustainability our competitive edge?"

Global leaders and industry experts consistently emphasise the urgent need for businesses to adopt sustainable practices—not just for the environment but for their own survival in a changing world. In this chapter, we will explore key lessons from pioneers in sustainability, drawing on their insights to inspire MSMEs and other businesses to embark on the path to sustainable growth.

MSMEs, in particular, have a tremendous opportunity to lead the charge toward sustainability. Their agility allows them to adapt faster than larger enterprises, making them well-positioned to capitalise on the emerging green economy. The question is no longer *whether* sustainability is essential, but *how* businesses can embed it deeply into their DNA.

Expert Insight: The Economics of Sustainability

One of the most persistent myths surrounding sustainability is that it is costly and detracts from profitability. Experts across industries have dispelled this notion, making it clear that the economics of sustainability work in favour of businesses that adopt it early.

The idea that **economics and the environment are at odds** is rapidly becoming outdated. Forward-thinking leaders now realise that **sustainability and profitability can go hand-in-hand**. For example, the integration of renewable energy sources like solar and wind not only reduces carbon emissions but also cuts energy costs over time. In fact, businesses that switch to renewable energy have reported reductions in energy expenses, which in turn boost their bottom line.

For MSMEs, the potential for cost savings through sustainability is even more significant. MSMEs that invest in energy-efficient technologies, optimise resource use, or switch to renewable energy sources often see **reduced operational costs** in the long-term. But the benefits don't stop there. By demonstrating a commitment to sustainability, MSMEs can also attract more customers, build stronger brand loyalty, and access new funding from investors who prioritise environmental, social, and governance (ESG) factors.

This lesson is particularly relevant in industries such as manufacturing and agriculture, where energy consumption and resource use are high. By taking steps to minimise waste and improve energy efficiency, MSMEs can build leaner, more profitable operations while reducing their environmental footprint.

The Power of Collaboration: Working Together for Greater Impact

Another key lesson from sustainability pioneers is the importance of **collaboration**. Businesses do not operate in isolation – they are part of a broader ecosystem that includes suppliers, customers, governments, and the community. Sustainable success, therefore, requires collaboration at every level.

MSMEs, with their limited resources, can often find it challenging to implement large-scale sustainability initiatives on their own. But by **partnering with other businesses**, industry groups, or NGOs, they can achieve greater results than they could alone. These partnerships can take many forms—shared renewable energy projects, joint investments in sustainable technologies, or collaborative supply chains that prioritise environmental responsibility.

One shining example of collaboration comes from the agriculture sector. Small farmers and MSMEs involved in organic farming often band together in cooperatives to share resources, reduce costs, and collectively market their sustainable produce. This not only makes sustainability more achievable but also increases the visibility of their products in the market. Through **collaborative networks**, businesses can scale their efforts, reach new markets, and increase their competitive advantage.

In the manufacturing industry, several small and medium-sized enterprises have collaborated to develop **green supply chains**, ensuring that their materials are sourced sustainably and their products are manufactured with minimal environmental impact. These efforts not only help reduce emissions but also strengthen relationships with clients who prioritise sustainability in their purchasing decisions.

Collaboration is also essential in navigating complex sustainability issues like carbon reduction and water management. For instance, by working together on **water conservation projects**, businesses in water-intensive industries can share the costs of implementing new technologies and make a greater impact collectively than they could individually.

The lesson here is clear: **sustainability is not a solo journey**. MSMEs that embrace collaboration will find that they can achieve far more by working with others than by going it alone. And in a world where sustainability is increasingly valued, these partnerships can be a key differentiator.

Innovation Through Sustainability: Embracing New Technologies

One of the most inspiring insights from sustainability leaders is the role of **innovation** in driving sustainable growth. For years, sustainability was seen as a constraint—a limit on what businesses could do. But today, it's recognised as a driver of **innovation and creativity**. Businesses that prioritise sustainability are more likely to embrace new technologies, improve processes, and create products that meet the evolving demands of the market.

For MSMEs, innovation is key to standing out in competitive markets. Sustainability presents an opportunity to differentiate not just by what you do, but by *how* you do it. Whether it's through the use of **renewable energy**, **waste reduction technologies**, or **digital tools** that monitor and optimise resource use, innovation is essential for MSMEs looking to lead in sustainability.

In manufacturing, for example, **energy-efficient technologies** such as automated systems that optimise production processes can drastically reduce energy consumption. By embracing these technologies, MSMEs can reduce both their costs and their carbon footprint. In agriculture, **precision farming technologies** that use sensors to monitor soil health, water use, and crop growth help farmers maximise yields while minimising environmental impact.

The shift towards sustainable innovation doesn't just benefit the environment—it opens up new market opportunities. Consumers are increasingly seeking out **eco-friendly products** and **sustainable solutions**, and businesses that can meet this demand are well-positioned for growth. Innovation also enables MSMEs to stay ahead of **regulatory changes**, ensuring that they comply with future environmental regulations while maintaining a competitive edge.

Building a Circular Economy: Reducing Waste and Maximising Resources

One of the most exciting concepts gaining traction in the sustainability world is the **circular economy**. Unlike the traditional linear economy, where resources are extracted, used, and then discarded, the circular economy focuses on **minimising waste** by keeping materials in use for as long as possible. This involves reusing, repairing, refurbishing, and recycling products and materials to create a closed-loop system.

For MSMEs, the transition to a circular economy presents a tremendous opportunity. By **rethinking product design** and **production processes**, businesses can reduce waste, lower costs, and create new revenue streams. For example, MSMEs in the textile industry are finding innovative ways to recycle fabric scraps into new products, turning what was once waste into valuable resources.

Manufacturers are also adopting **circular business models** by designing products that are easier to disassemble and repair, extending their lifecycle and reducing the need for new raw materials. This not only reduces the environmental impact of production but also creates new business opportunities in repair services and product take-back schemes.

Another key aspect of the circular economy is **waste-to-energy** technologies, where waste materials are converted into energy. This is particularly valuable for businesses in industries like agriculture and food processing, where organic waste can be transformed into biogas or other forms of renewable energy. By turning waste into a resource, MSMEs can reduce disposal costs and contribute to a cleaner energy future.

The shift to a circular economy is not just a trend—it's a necessity for businesses looking to thrive in a resource-constrained world. MSMEs that embrace circular practices will be better equipped to navigate the challenges of resource scarcity while gaining a competitive edge in sustainable markets.

Long-Term Strategy: Building Sustainability into Your Core Business Model

Perhaps the most important lesson from sustainability pioneers is the need for businesses to **embed sustainability into their core business strategy**. Sustainability cannot be an afterthought or a side project. It needs to be deeply integrated into every aspect of a business, from product design and supply chains to customer engagement and corporate governance.

For MSMEs, this means **thinking long-term**. It's about moving beyond short-term gains and focusing on the long-term health of both the business and the planet. By adopting a long-term sustainability strategy, businesses can ensure that they are not only meeting the demands of today but also preparing for the challenges of tomorrow.

A key part of this strategy involves setting **measurable sustainability goals** and tracking progress over time. Whether it's reducing carbon emissions, conserving water, or cutting waste, businesses need to establish clear objectives and regularly assess their performance. This not only helps ensure accountability but also allows businesses to communicate their sustainability achievements to customers, investors, and other stakeholders.

Another important aspect of building sustainability into your business model is **engaging your workforce**. Employees are often the best advocates for sustainability initiatives, and businesses that involve their teams in the journey towards sustainability are more likely to succeed. By fostering a culture of innovation and responsibility, MSMEs can inspire their employees to take ownership of sustainability efforts, driving greater results.

Actionable Steps for MSMEs to Build a Sustainable Future

So, how can MSMEs take these lessons and apply them to their own sustainability journey? Here are some actionable steps that businesses can take to start building a more sustainable future:

1. Conduct a Sustainability Audit

Start by conducting a comprehensive sustainability audit of your business. Identify areas where you can reduce energy consumption, minimise waste, and optimise resource use. This audit will serve as the foundation for your sustainability strategy, helping you prioritise initiatives and measure progress.

2. Invest in Green Technologies

As part of your sustainability strategy, look for opportunities to invest in **green technologies** that reduce your environmental impact. Whether it's renewable energy solutions, energy-efficient machinery, or waste reduction technologies, these investments will help you cut costs and improve your sustainability performance.

3. Collaborate with Partners

Sustainability is a collaborative effort, and MSMEs can achieve greater results by working with partners. Collaborate with other businesses, NGOs, and industry groups to share resources, reduce costs, and scale your sustainability initiatives.

4. Engage Customers and Investors

Don't keep your sustainability efforts to yourself. Communicate your progress to customers, investors, and other stakeholders. Share the story of your sustainability journey and demonstrate the positive impact your business is making on the environment.

5. Set Long-Term Goals

Sustainability is a long-term commitment. Set ambitious but achievable sustainability goals for your business and regularly assess your progress. By staying focused on the long-term, you'll ensure that sustainability remains a core part of your business strategy.

Call to Action: Lead the Charge Towards a Sustainable Future

The path to a sustainable future is clear, but the journey requires commitment, innovation, and collaboration. MSMEs have the unique opportunity to lead the charge towards a more sustainable economy. By adopting green practices, investing in innovation, and building sustainability into their core business model, MSMEs can thrive in a world that increasingly values environmental responsibility.

The time to act is now. Start by taking small steps, engage with your partners and stakeholders, and set ambitious goals for your business. By doing so, you'll not only contribute to a more sustainable world but also position your business for long-term success.

Let's build a future where sustainability and profitability go hand-in-hand – and let MSMEs be the leaders of this transformation.

Acknowledgements

This book represents not just my journey but the collective wisdom, encouragement, and expertise of many remarkable individuals who have inspired me to document the essential qualities of *Planecious* leaders. Their insights into sustainable practices and accountability have shaped not only this book but also my own understanding of what it means to lead with purpose. I am deeply grateful to the mentors and visionaries whose guidance and belief in this project made it possible.

- **Sunny Revankar:** Your deep expertise in ESG reporting, sustainable finance, and corporate governance has been foundational to Chapters 1 and 2. Your leadership at Stirrup Communications and your ability to navigate the complexities of frameworks like SEBI's BRSR (Business Responsibility and Sustainability Reporting) guidelines provided invaluable context and clarity.

- **Soumitra Purkayastha:** Your dedication to fostering inclusive leadership and innovation within the chemical industry profoundly shaped Chapter 3. Your story exemplifies how sustainability and leadership can intersect to create lasting change.

- **Saurabh Mehta**: Thank you for your pioneering work in creating the world's first plastic-free pen, a journey that has redefined what zero-waste innovation looks like. Chapter 4 is a testament to your vision and perseverance in tackling environmental challenges head-on.

- **Mohammed Mahmoud**: Your contributions to climate adaptation and water management were pivotal in Chapter 5. Your ability to balance economic development with sustainability highlights the importance of cross-disciplinary collaboration in addressing global challenges.

- **Karunakar Avuram**: Your work in energy efficiency and renewable energy projects, particularly with organisations like Godrej and Mahindra, provided key insights for Chapters 6 and 7. Your leadership in integrating circular economy principles has inspired countless businesses to adopt sustainable practices.

- **Erik Solheim**: Your unique perspective on the New Green Economy and the future of renewable energy was instrumental in Chapter 7. Your experience as a former UN Environment Executive added a global dimension to this book's exploration of sustainability.

- **Dr. Aditi Mishal**: Thank you for your groundbreaking work on sustainable development and the Smart Toilet Tracking System. Chapter 8 showcases how technological innovation can address critical public infrastructure challenges sustainably.

- **Ankur Vaidya**: Your leadership with the Federation of Indian Associations brought to life the potential of grassroots movements in Chapter 10. Thank you for illustrating how community initiatives can align with sustainability goals.

- **Dr. Jaimin Vasa, Shri Jagdish Vishwakarma, Dr. Neerja Gupta, Jagat Kinkhabwala, Arya Patel, and Pankaj Patel**: Your expertise in MSMEs and the carbon credit market greatly informed Chapter 13. The insights you shared during the Environmental Sustainability programme at Gujarat University were instrumental in highlighting the role of small businesses in global sustainability efforts.

I also want to express my gratitude to the companies referenced throughout this book, such as Godrej, Mahindra, Tata, and Accenture. Their forward-thinking leadership in ESG and sustainability initiatives provided real-world examples that illuminate the transformative potential of sustainable business practices.

My coaches and mentors have been a guiding force throughout this journey. Their wisdom, encouragement, and support have been invaluable. Many individuals have contributed to shaping and bringing this book to life, and to them, I extend my deepest appreciation. To my Gracia Marcom team, who supported me at every step, and to my family and my business partner, Nirali Korat, who were enthusiastic and responsive to my needs, I owe a heartfelt thanks. To my publisher, Notion Press, and their dedicated team, your efforts in shaping the manuscript have brought this vision to life.

This book is a testament to the collective efforts of everyone who believes in a sustainable future. My deepest gratitude goes out to all who have played a part in bringing this project to fruition.

Notes

This section provides the sources for key statistics, case studies, interviews, and examples mentioned throughout the book:

1. **ESG Reporting and SEBI's BRSR: Chapters 1 and 2** draw on the expertise of **Sunny Revankar**, who explained the implications of **SEBI's BRSR guidelines** for top 1000 listed companies in India. His work at **Stirrup Communications** helped businesses navigate the shift from traditional financial reporting to integrating **ESG metrics**.

2. **Sustainable Innovation in the Chemical Industry: Soumitra Purkayastha's** leadership in the chemical industry and his focus on **inclusive innovation** was a central theme of **Chapter 3**, demonstrating how sustainability can drive both business growth and social impact.

3. **Plastic-Free Pen and Zero-Waste Innovation: Saurabh Mehta's** creation of the world's first **plastic-free pen**, discussed in **Chapter 4**, serves as a case study on how small-scale eco-entrepreneurship can contribute to global sustainability efforts.

4. **Water Management and Climate Adaptation: Mohammed Mahmoud's** contributions to **Chapter**

5 focused on balancing economic development with sustainable water management strategies, addressing the global challenges of water scarcity.

5. **Energy Efficiency and Circular Economy:** **Karunakar Avuram's** work on energy audits in **Godrej's** operations and the adoption of circular economy principles in **Mahindra** were key discussions in **Chapters 6 and 7**. His efforts contributed to reducing emissions and enhancing sustainability in large-scale industries.

6. **Renewable Energy in the New Green Economy:** **Erik Solheim's** global perspective on the future of **renewable energy** and the **New Green Economy** was instrumental in **Chapter 7**. His insights as a former diplomat have influenced global sustainability strategies.

7. **Smart Infrastructure Solutions:** Dr. **Aditi Mishal's** work on the **Smart Toilet Tracking System**, detailed in **Chapter 8**, is an example of how technological innovation can address critical infrastructure challenges while promoting sustainability.

8. **Community-Led Sustainability:** **Ankur Vaidya's** leadership with the **Federation of Indian Associations**, discussed in **Chapter 10**, demonstrated the importance of community-driven sustainability efforts.

9. **Carbon Credits for MSMEs:** Dr. **Jaimin Vasa's** insights into how **MSMEs** can leverage **carbon credits** to drive both sustainability and profitability were central to **Chapter 16**.

10. **Digital Transformation in Sustainability**: **Accenture's** study, referenced in **Chapter** 7, indicated that digital technologies can reduce a company's emissions by up to 20%, while also improving operational efficiency.

11. **ESG as a Driver of Investment**: A study by **Deloitte**, cited in **Chapters 7 and 8**, found that 79% of global investors consider **ESG factors** in their decision-making process.

Bibliography

Godrej Consumer Products Ltd.: https://www.godrejcp.com/sustainability

CII Green Business Centre http://www.greenbusinesscentre.com/

Mahindra: https://www.mahindra.com/rise/sustainability

Tata: https://www.tatasustainability.com/

Accenture: https://www.accenture.com/dk-en/services/sustainability

Deloitte: https://www.deloitte.com/global/en/issues/climate/sustainability-and-climate.html

UN: United Nations https://www.unwater.org/water-facts/water-scarcity, https://www.un.org/en/global-issues/water

Harvard Business Review: https://hbr.org/2016/10/the-comprehensive-business-case-for-sustainability

MIT's Media Lab: The MIT Media Lab is a research laboratory at the Massachusetts Institute of Technology https://www.media.mit.edu/

Kyoto Protocol. https://unfccc.int/kyoto_protocol

International Energy Agency (IEA). https://www.iea.org/

COP28, or the 28th United Nations Climate Change Conference https://unfccc.int/cop28

NOTE: No Offence to Earth. https://thenote.earth/

MSCI: https://www.msci.com

BRSR: Business Responsibility & Sustainability Reporting. https://www.sebi.gov.in/

GRI: Global Reporting Initiative. https://www.globalreporting.org/

SASB: Sustainability Accounting Standards Board. https://sasb.ifrs.org/

SEBI: Securities and Exchange Board of India. https://www.sebi.gov.in/

CDP: Carbon Disclosure Project. https://www.cdp.net/en